PALLET STYLE

NIKKITA PALMER and **BILLY BARKER**
are up-and-coming young designers. They
design bespoke furniture and homewares
for domestic interiors, retail stores and cafés,
with stockists across the UK. Nikkita is a
regular contributor to *Open Air* magazine
and *The Glamping Magazine*, and often
features on lifestyle blogs with both her
furniture and hire collections.

PALLET STYLE

20 creative home projects
using recycled wooden pallets

**NIKKITA PALMER
& BILLY BARKER**

Photography by Brent Darby

KYLE BOOKS

*In loving memory of Grandad Ian
and Grandad Palmer xx*

An Hachette UK Company
www.hachette.co.uk

First published in Great Britain in 2019 by
Kyle Books, an imprint of Kyle Cathie Ltd
Carmelite House
50 Victoria Embankment
London EC4Y 0DZ
www.kylebooks.co.uk

ISBN: 978 0 857835222

Distributed in the US by Hachette Book Group, 1290 Avenue
of the Americas,
4th and 5th Floors, New York, NY 10104

Distributed in Canada by Canadian Manda Group, 664
Annette St., Toronto, Ontario, Canada M6S 2C8

Publisher: Joanna Copestick
Editor: Tara O'Sullivan
Editorial Assistant: Isabel Gonzalez-Prendergast
Design: Rachel Cross
Photography: Brent Darby
Props styling: Agathe Gits
Production: Lucy Carter

A Cataloguing in Publication record for this title is available
from the British Library

Printed and bound in China

10 9 8 7 6 5 4 3 2 1

A NOTE ON MEASUREMENTS

Dimensions and measurements in this book are
given in both metric and imperial. Please follow
one system consistently and do not combine
the two.

CONTENTS

INTRODUCTION

HELLO

Firstly, welcome and thank you for picking up our book, we are absolutely thrilled you are here! Having learned and experienced so much in our time building Nikkita Palmer Designs, we are honoured, excited and eager to share our lovingly made projects with you straight from our workshop and studio in the Bedfordshire countryside. With my background in textile design and Billy's in the boating industry, together we combine and create with a balance of design, craftsmanship and functionality. Along with our little dog Maddie, we spend our days creating and designing in our studio and our weekends foraging, finding and collecting. On the following pages you will find an array of designs and products that we have put together to create the perfect chic interior made entirely from pallets and reclaimed materials.

WHY PALLETS?

From a young age I have been surrounded by the use of reclaimed wood and material, a then not-so-fashionable concept. My stepdad, who works in the concreting industry, would bring home the wood that would otherwise be discarded from their shipped supplies. Both my brother and I would earn our pocket money dismantling and removing nails from pallet boards to use in household makes and furniture projects – something I never dreamed I would still be doing 20 years on!

From selling upcycled projects to earn enough money to go to university, I then became more involved and interested in the interior trend industry. My graduate collection was focused around sustainability and in particular Biophilic design, a concept that promotes the use of natural materials in the built environment in order to increase productivity as well as mental and physical wellbeing.

I continued this focus when I created my design company with my partner Billy, and combined my love of Biophilic design with the use of pallets and other reclaimed material. With the use of natural materials now so popular within interiors, both commercially and in the home, pallet wood lends itself by not only being (mostly) free but also really effective when used in the right ways.

Pallets are known to be the single most important object of the global economy. Used to transport goods throughout the world, they have become a common sight in our ever-growing consumerist society. It is estimated that there are over 10 billion pallets in use at any one time, with the majority of these sent directly to landfill after use. With the occasional DIYer seeing a pallet as a cheap alternative to pricey store-bought material, the pallet for us is sustainable, versatile and aesthetically beautiful – a perfect combination!

USING THIS BOOK

Creating a picture-perfect space really doesn't need to be expensive. This book is full of beautiful and practical pieces that can be adapted and reinvented to fit a variety of styles and personalities. In our over-saturated, technology-driven world, as humans, we long for a deeper connection to the natural world around us. As consumerism continues to suffocate our lives with products we don't really need, we begin to crave an authentic connection with the products we own, use and interact with. What better way to achieve this than by building them ourselves?

Through the use of reclaimed, natural materials and the process of making, these projects are designed to be used and loved. Your creations will be full of character and lend style to your space, whether you go all out and make a pallet sofa, or simply use reclaimed wood from pallets to build a striking herb planter. We encourage you, throughout this book, to push boundaries, think outside the box and be influenced by the things and people around you. Be creative and don't be afraid – I promise you, even the best makers make mistakes!

PALLETS - THE BASICS

The content of this book is based on our own personal experiences, and while we want you to learn and develop your skills, all the materials and measurements will vary depending on what you have access to. We encourage you to find, forage and reuse as much as you can in the process of making and you will find the materials you collect will also determine the techniques or processes you use.

SOURCING

While some individuals and businesses sell pallets, many are looking to give them away for free. The internet can be a good source, with many selling sites, Freecycle groups and social media groups now hosting an abundance of free pallet posts. While you should always ask permission before taking pallets, industrial sites are great if you're looking for a bigger stock or a variety of sizes. With most businesses now having to pay to get pallets removed, many will happily give them away for little or no money.

NOTE: Always ask permission before taking any materials that do not belong to you.

TYPES OF PALLETS

When choosing your pallet consider your finished item – think about the size, weight and appearance you're looking for. Industrial sites are good for sourcing longer pallets, which we love as they allow you to make table tops and

bigger furniture without using smaller pieces, giving a more professional finish. Euro pallets tend to be much harder to deconstruct, however they are great for projects like the planter on page 108, and those that use whole pallets. We also use the blocks from these to create tea light holders (see page 150). Some pallets allow you to use everything. The centre supports on two-way entry, or stringer, pallets (referred to as pallet bearers or stringers), for example, make great structural supports or chunky uprights and table legs. This type of pallet is also usually easier to take apart.

There are six internationally recognised standard sizes for pallets, but the most common one used in North America is 1219 x 1016mm (48 x 40in). In the UK a two-way entry pallet is usually 1200 x 1000mm (47¼ x 39½in), with a full-perimeter base – this evolved in the 1960s as the closest metric equivalent to the standard American size. The Euro is 800 x 1200mm (31½ x 47¼in), and is designed to fit through most standard doorways.

When using more than one pallet on a project, be sure to check the thickness of each pallet board, as this can vary. This can be resolved with planing and lots of sanding, but it always looks best if the pallets are a consistent thickness to begin with. There is a concern within the pallet furniture industry about the

potential spillage of chemical and unknown substances on pallet wood. To avoid this, be sure to use pallets with 'HT' stamped on them. This refers to a 'Heat Treated' finish, which is used to kill and remove any unwanted chemicals, bugs or plant diseases in the pallet. These pallets are used within the food industry, among many others.

Bearer/Stringer beams

Throughout the projects in this book we use the pallet bearer and stringer beams as well as the pallet boards. The bearer/stringer beams are sourced from a two-way entry or stringer pallet. They consist of a chunkier material (in a range of sizes) that supports the pallet boards and are great for structural beams in the larger makes. While we always try our best to source two-way entry/stringer pallets, an alternative is to use scaffolding boards cut down to length on a table saw. This creates a similar beam that can be used in the same way. Alternatively, contact warehouses and industrial areas as they regularly get larger stock delivered on big singular support beams rather than pallets. These are particularly good for the headboard on page 18 and the table and bench legs on page 66 and 78.

Scaffold boards

A few of the projects in the book use reclaimed scaffold boards and while these are a great material they can have their issues. Primarily used in the building industry, scaffold boards can often carry a lot of moisture internally. We always

advise that you leave the boards in a warm room (central-heated is best) until they are completely dry – this can sometimes take up to six weeks. Failure to let the boards dry out will result in them shrinking and expanding once the project is assembled and placed in a centrally heated home, leaving unwanted gaps and splits.

DECONSTRUCTION OF A PALLET

There are several ways to take apart a pallet to get the best results. Here are some of the techniques we prefer to use. When deconstructing a pallet, be sure to use appropriate protective clothing, such as gloves and eyewear. Always lay the pallet on a flat surface for this process.

Claw hammer

Use the claw of your hammer to sit under the centre of your pallet board at the connecting joints and lever up. Continue this at both ends until the board becomes loose. If you struggle with the amount of leverage, try using a crow bar to help you. If your pallet has blocks or support beams on the base, knocking these off with your hammer is another option, but this could damage the beams.

Hand saw and claw hammer

A slightly easier technique is to cut the pallet boards on the inside of the end blocks, using a hand saw and a combination square to ensure a straight cut. Once the board is loose at either end, use the claw hammer or crow bar to lever the centre of the board loose.

If your project consists of smaller pieces of pallet wood, you can cut at every block on the pallet with a hand saw, leaving smaller nail-free pieces. Depending on the size of the pallet, this may work for the shelving project on page 96.

Lifting bar

Our favourite and easiest technique is to use a lifting bar (also called a pallet breaker or pallet buster). This is a more advanced form of a crow bar that simply sits under each connecting joint and levers the board free from the supporting beams or blocks. They can be purchased online or at larger tool stores.

Removing nails

You can simply do this with a claw hammer, using the claw to straighten any bent nails, knocking them through and removing them on the opposite side with the claw. However, I prefer to use a set of pliers or wire snips to aid this process. It not only allows you to straighten the nails more quickly and easily, it also enables you to cut off any nails that refuse to straighten and to extract nails more easily once they are knocked through.

PERFECTING YOUR PALLET BOARDS

Here are just a few things we suggest you do to your pallet boards before you start making. Although not essential, they will give a better end result.

Trimming: Using reclaimed material can mean that the wood often has imperfections, such as twists, warps and knots. We trim the long edge of every pallet board we use, which allows the boards to sit flush to each other on the finished product. We do this on a table saw

which, once set up, does the job swiftly and accurately. This can also be achieved by sanding, but does take more time.

Cutting your ends: We always cut the ends of our pallet boards straight. Using reclaimed material can mean that not everything is square on the board so it is always best to recut before measuring for your project. This also results in a nice little pile of kindling from your ends.

Marking: When measuring the pallet boards, always use a combination square to mark a line. This will ensure you always get a straight cut.

Sanding: Reclaimed timber, especially pallet wood, can be very rough and time consuming to get perfectly smooth. We suggest you always use an electric sander and good-quality sandpaper – this may cost more, but will last longer and result in a much better finish. Start your sanding with a coarse grit such as 80 to remove most of the unwanted material, then finish with a finer grit such as 120 (or higher) to give a smooth finish. If you don't have an electric sander, use the same process by hand. Be patient with sanding; although it may take time, the finished result will be worth it. Be sure to always wear an appropriate ventilation mask when sanding, and carry it out in a well-ventilated room.

ESSENTIAL TOOLS & TECHNIQUES

Pilot hole: It is important to always create a pilot hole using an electric drill and a drill bit appropriately sized for your screw before screwing, especially when working with reclaimed/pallet wood as it has a tendency to split and crack. Piloting will give a guide for the screw, so will reduce or avoid any splitting and give a cleaner finish.

Countersink: A countersink can be created in several ways, with a countersink tool that fits into an electric drill or by using a larger drill bit. A countersink is used to enlarge and bevel the rim of the pilot hole so that the screw sits flush with the surface when drilled, giving a more professional finish.

Doweling: We regularly dowel the countersunk hole after screwing to neaten and give a cleaner finish. Using an appropriate-sized dowel to the countersink (usually around 9mm/ $5/16$in), dip a small piece of dowel into wood glue (the dowel needs to be longer than the hole). Knock it into the countersunk hole with a hammer. Once dry, cut off any excess dowel with a hand saw (if needed) and sand until flush with the surface of the wood. Note: you may need a deeper countersink to allow for dowelling.

Combination Square: A combination square is essential when measuring and marking, as it provides a 90° straight edge.

FURNITURE

With our homes becoming smaller, more versatile spaces, furniture is becoming less static and more multi-purpose and moveable. Quality takes the lead from quantity as we strive for practical yet beautiful spaces which enhance our busy lives. The following projects prove how achievable it is to create the basics of the home entirely from reclaimed materials. In both a beautiful and stylish way, these pallet projects can create the bones of a space, whether that be an apartment, family home or small-space alternative.

PLATFORM BED

Although one of the larger projects in the book, our platform pallet bed is the most simple and can be carried out by all abilities. Perfect for those starting out in new and first homes, this bed is super cheap and can look really effective. Using whole pallets as a base gives the opportunity to experiment with many designs. Try including stepped platforms to give more height, or using the hollow cavities to store shoes or books. Having recently moved from our tiny boat and with little income to spare, Billy and I made one of these for our own room, which looks great. Not only is this design practical and simple, but it gets lots of compliments from anyone who sees it. Our main advice for this project is to ensure all of the pallets are the same height and style to give an even and secure surface. These are easier to source from industrial sites where they only deal with one kind of product. If you like, you can swap the headboard for the overbed shelves on page 102.

———

TOOLS AND EQUIPMENT

TAPE MEASURE

PILOT DRILL BIT

COUNTERSINK DRILL BIT

ELECTRIC DRILL

SCREW-DRIVER BIT

ELECTRIC SANDER AND SANDPAPER

VENTILATION MASK

COMBINATION SQUARE

HAND SAW OR TABLE SAW

PAINT BRUSH

MATERIALS

4 IDENTICAL PALLETS (THE TOTAL
    DIMENSION MUST BE BIG ENOUGH
    TO FIT YOUR CHOSEN MATTRESS), PLUS
    EXTRA PALLET BOARDS TO FILL IN GAPS
    IF NEEDED

CONNECTOR PLATES

WOOD SCREWS

9 INDUSTRIAL CASTORS (2-4 LOCKABLE)

40MM (1½IN) PANEL PINS

OSB (ORIENTED STRAND BOARD)

GREY CHALK PAINT

4 SPRING HEAD NAILS OR COPPER
    CLOUT NAILS

01

To prepare the pallet boards, please refer to Perfecting your Pallet Boards on page 12.

01 Lay four identical pallets (underside facing up) on a flat surface to create the main base structure. Ours came to 239 x 159.5cm (95 x 63in) (see note under 'Materials').

02 Attach the pallets together at the blocks by making a pilot hole and countersink in each one. Using an electric drill and screwdriver bit, screw the pallets together using long screws.

03 You can also attach flat connector plates to the centre to strengthen further.

Fill in any gaps on the pallets with additional pallet boards. Ensure there is a dense structure to give strength to the base.

04 Secure 3 castors on each of the top and bottom edges and 3 more along the centre using an electric drill, screwdriver bit and screws. Try to attach these to the pallet blocks to give additional strength, and position the lockable castors diagonally opposite each other.

02

03

04

We salvaged some of our castors, so they aren't all the same size. We just attached blocks of wood to the smaller ones to give the same height.

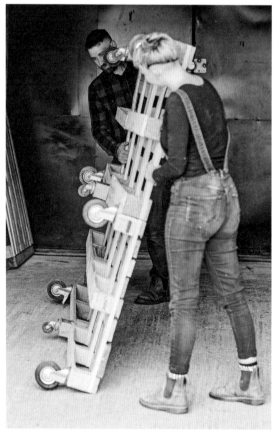

05

06

05 Turn the entire structure so that the castors are on the floor.

06 Lock the castors to reduce movement and sand all of the pallets to remove splinters.

07

08

09

07 Measure, mark and cut two industrial bearer/stringer beams at 90cm (35in) and one at 159.5cm (63in) or the width of your bed. These will create the headboard. Sand the beams.

Secure the two 90cm (35in) beams to either end of the top edge of the pallet using an electric drill, pilot, countersink, screwdriver bit and screws to create the headboard uprights.

08 Place the remaining beam on the top of the two shorter beams, ensuring they're flush at both ends. Secure using an electric drill, pilot bit, countersink, screwdriver bit and screws.

09 Cut the OSB board with a table saw/handsaw at 30cm (1ft) wide. Cut the length of the OSB at 159.5cm (63in) or the width of your bed. Sand the OSB to give a smoother finish. Paint with a grey chalk paint to create the chalkboard. Decide where you would like your chalkboard to sit on the headboard and measure and mark down the headboard to ensure it is level.

10 Attach the OSB at each corner to the side beams on the headboard with spring-head nails to add an industrial decoration. Decorate the headboard with chalkboard pens.

10

HOME BAR

Whether in the garden or kitchen, at a wedding or festival, this bar is perfect for entertaining guests. Our clients have used and adapted this design for a variety of purposes around the home, from covering kitchen appliances to housing speaker systems and glassware. Our inspiration for this came from the idea of wedding welcome drinks on hot summer days in big flowered gardens, and this piece now sits among our hire collection for events. With chalkboard signage for personalisation you can use the bar for special events, witty notes and family messages, whether paired with vintage cake stands and crockery, bottles of botanical gin and cocktail glasses, or drinks dispensers and fruit juices – the choice is yours.

TOOLS AND EQUIPMENT

TAPE MEASURE

PENCIL

COMBINATION SQUARE

HAND SAW OR ELECTRIC CHOP/MITRE SAW

PILOT DRILL BIT

COUNTERSINK DRILL BIT

ELECTRIC DRILL

SCREWDRIVER BIT

ELECTRIC SANDER AND SANDPAPER

VENTILATION MASK

HAMMER

GOOD-QUALITY MASKING TAPE

PAINT BRUSH

JIGSAW (OPTIONAL)

CLAMPS

CLOTH OR BRUSH FOR OIL

MATERIALS

17 PALLET BEARER/STRINGER BEAMS FROM A
    TWO-WAY ENTRY PALLET (WE CUT OURS IN
    HALF TO MAKE BEST USE OF THE MATERIAL)

WOOD SCREWS

60 PALLET BOARDS (APPROX.)

1 WIDE PALLET BOARD

WOOD GLUE

PANEL PINS (40MM/1½IN)

CHALKBOARD PAINT

DANISH OIL (OPTIONAL)

To prepare the pallet boards, please refer to Perfecting your Pallet Boards on page 12.

FRAME:

01 Measure, mark and cut 3 beams at 33cm (13in) and 2 beams at 100cm (40in).

Place two 33cm (13in) beams on the inside of each end of the two longer beams. Pilot two screw holes into each beam end from the side of the longer beams. Countersink the pilot holes and screw into the middle beams.

02 Repeat until they are attached at each end to make a rectangular frame.

03 Measure from the inside edge of each end and mark a centre point. Mark the centre of the final 33cm (13in) beam. Align with the centre point on the frame and slot into the centre. Pilot, countersink and screw as before, from the outside edge.

Repeat the steps above to make a second frame exactly the same way.

04 Measure, mark and cut 7 beams at 90cm (35in). These are your uprights. Pilot, countersink and screw 4 of the beams to each corner of the frames made in steps 1 to 3 by screwing down into the ends of the uprights.

05 When you are finished, you will have completed a 3D rectangular frame.

01

02

03

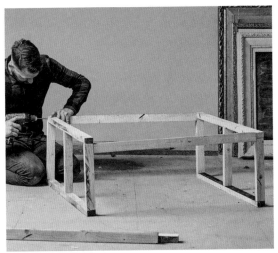

04

05

06

06 Measure and mark the centre of one long edge of the frame at both ends. Place another upright on the mark and screw from the top and bottom frames to create a centre support at the front of the bar.

07 Repeat on the two smaller side panels. These supports will help when cladding the bar. Sand the entire frame to give a smooth finish.

BAR SIGNAGE

08 Cut two beams at 185cm (72in). Add three pilot and countersink holes into the beams to attach to the bar frame. Screw both the beams into either end of the bar frame.

09 Cut a wide pallet board at 100cm (40in). Clamp to the top of the two uprights created in step 8 to hold into position. Pilot, countersink and screw the pallet board into position from the back.

Sand the signage board and uprights.

10 Measure and mark a rectangle in the centre of the pallet board, 6cm (2½in) in from the ends and 3cm (1in) in from the top and bottom.

11 Mask using good-quality masking tape. and paint using chalkboard paint and a paint brush.

07

08

09

10

11

12

13

14

PALLET CLADDING

You will need a lot of pallet boards here. It is always best to trim the boards down each side before attaching, especially when they are to sit flush as in this project (see Perfecting your Pallet Boards page 12).

12 Start with the shorter side panels, measuring and cutting each one to size. They need to be long enough to also cover the bar sign uprights.

13 Apply wood glue to the frame. Attach pallet boards with pin nails and a hammer.

Note: you only need to clad the front (of the longer sides) as the other acts as the back and additional storage. You may have boards that fit the entire length of the front or you may need two. Try to alternate so that half boards always sit between two full boards for the best effect. Use the centre beam on the front (created in step 6) to attach half boards.

14 Repeat the same process with the front and top, ensuring you make the pallet boards slightly longer (always measure) than the frame in order to cover the ends of the side boards. This gives a neat finish. Now sand the entire bar (it is best to use an electric sander here) to get a smooth finish.

INSIDE BOTTOM SHELF

15 Now we'll create custom boards cut to the exact shapes you'll need to build a bottom shelf inside your bar. Measure from one side of the inside of the bar to the other. Measure, mark and cut a piece of pallet board to its length. Now measure around the support beams and mark these measurements onto the pallet board back corners using a pencil and combination square.

Cut out these small squares using a jigsaw or hand saw and slot the board into place.

Now cut another piece of pallet board to the length of the inside of the bar. Measure the distance between the previously placed board and the next support beam and, again, mark and cut the board to fit the space around the beam.

16 Continue in this manner until the base of the bar is complete. Glue and hammer the base boards into position with panel pin nails. Sand the entire shelf base. Although not essential, we love to use Danish oil to finish our pieces. For outdoor bars, finish with a varnish and re-apply at least once a year.

SOFA/DAY BED

While pallet seating has been continually popular, we've opted for a more stylish and adaptable alternative. Looking to remove the chunkiness of traditional pallet seating designs, we have used pallets solely for the base of the project. Combined with castors, scaffold-pole and hand-rail connectors, this project is less dense in its structure, adding a subtle but on-trend feature to both indoor and outdoor spaces. Using a single mattress for the base cushion means that this sofa also doubles up perfectly as a guest bed. It is suited to student households, modern apartments, teenage hangouts or garden patios, and you can adapt the designs, fabrics and size to make it personal to you. Although simple in its construction, this project uses more advanced tools, with a grinder needed to cut the pole, so we would always recommend this is carried out by someone more experienced, and using the correct tools and safety wear.

TOOLS AND EQUIPMENT

TAPE MEASURE

VENTILATION MASK

PILOT DRILL BIT

COUNTERSINK DRILL BIT

ELECTRIC DRILL

SCREWDRIVER BIT

HAMMER AND NAILS

GRINDER AND METAL CUTTING DISC

GOGGLES, A DUST MASK AND GLOVES

ALLEN KEY (SIZE OF HAND RAIL FIXINGS)

ELECTRIC SANDER AND SANDPAPER

MATERIALS

2 PALLETS

48MM (2IN) SCAFFOLD POLES, TOTAL
   LENGTH APPROX. 750CM/24FT 6IN

8 ELBOW 48MM (2IN) HAND RAIL
   CONNECTORS

8 WALL PLATE 48MM (2IN) HAND RAIL
   CONNECTORS

WOOD SCREWS

6 INDUSTRIAL CASTORS (2-4 LOCKABLE)

6-8 PIECES OF PALLET BOARD, PLUS
   ADDITIONAL BOARDS IF NEEDED

01

To prepare the pallet boards, please refer to Perfecting your Pallet Boards on page 12.

01 Join two pallets together. Ours made an overall length (when joined) of 240.5cm (7ft 10in) and a width of 100cm (3ft). Make sure your total dimensions are large enough to fit a single mattress with space around the edges. If the pallets do not have enough slats on the flat top side, add additional ones in the gaps from another pallet. This ensures that the entire structure is strong enough.

Position the pallets so that the underside is the working area. Pilot and countersink into the blocks, which sit together. Screw into the holes using an electric drill and screwdriver bit to secure the two pallets together. You will need long screws for this.

02

03

02 Continuing on the underside, secure six castors – one at each corner and two on the outer middle edges – using an electric drill, screwdriver bit and screws. Where possible try to attach to the blocks to give additional strength, and position the lockable castors diagonally opposite each other.

03 Turn the structure over so that the castors are on the floor and lock them in position. Place the single mattress in the centre of the sofa structure so that it sits flush with the front of the pallets, leaving a gap behind it and equal space to either side. Measure the space to either side of the mattress.

04 Measure, mark and cut pieces of pallet boards to these measurements. Nail (or screw if necessary) these pieces of wood into place –these will form your side tables.

04

05

06

05 Measure the gap to the back of the mattress and between the two side panels to determine the size of the back pallet boards.

06 Measure, mark and cut the boards, nailing or screwing into position as before.

07 Screw four of the wall plate connectors into the pallet board side tables. These should sit flush with the inside edge of the side boards and at the front and back. Screw the remaining two wall plate connectors at either end of the boards at the back as shown.

07

08 Using a grinder, cutting disc and appropriate safety wear, cut four scaffold pole lengths at 65cm (25in) and two poles to 75cm (30in).

09 Fit the four 65cm (25in) poles into the wall plates secured on the side tables, and the two longer poles into the wall plates secured on to the back boards. Those on the side tables will begin to form the arms of the sofa, and those on the back boards will form the back.

10 Attach the elbow connectors onto the top of the poles. Working your way around the sofa, measure between each set of two poles at their base to get the centre measurement and cut a pole to the right length for each set. Slot these poles into the elbow connectors to create the centre of each structure. Tighten the poles to secure using an allen key.

08

09

10

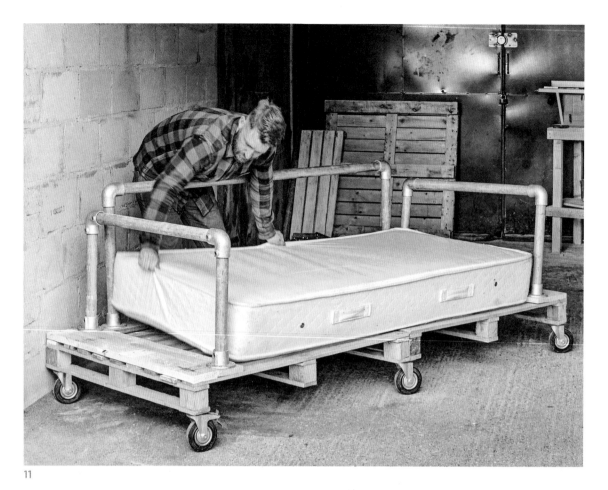

11

11 Sand the whole structure until smooth. Position the mattress on the sofa base, and cover with a fitted sheet. Pile up large cushions for the back and arms of the sofas and settle in.

TOP TIPS:

Use a single mattress as the cushion for the sofa and cover with a fitted sheet, which also enables easy washing and is simple to change with colour schemes.

If needed, you can also attach flat connector plates onto the join of the pallets underneath to strengthen.

If you cannot source cushions large enough for the back of the sofa, you can add another horizontal pole into the back, halfway up, with T-connectors to add support, or source custom sized cushion foam online.

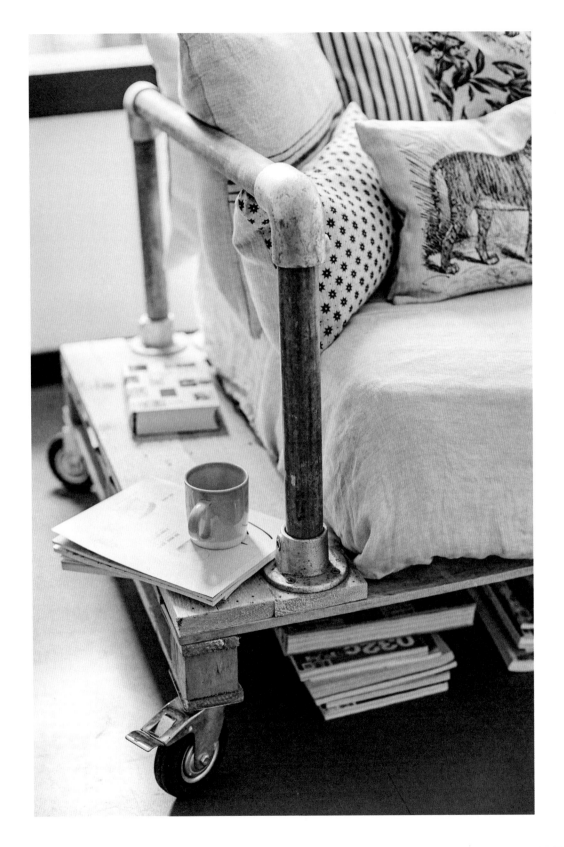

ROOM DIVIDER

This multi-use room divider is a stylish addition to studio apartments or open-plan living areas. Made from whole pallets and industrial castors, it not only provides a storage system but is also portable from room to room. With shelves on both sides, you can create a feature wall with images, books and handy household items. We use our room divider in the studio to separate my office area from our show room and find it a great visual centrepiece to the space. Another option for this project, and one that is on my never-ending list of jobs, is to use it in the garden. Grow plants up the pallets, through the gaps or use it to house potted plants, herbs and flowers. Not only would this create a feature piece in your outdoor space but it would also be great to separate seating areas from the rest of the garden.

TOOLS AND EQUIPMENT

HAND SAW

ELECTRIC SANDER AND SANDPAPER

PAINT BRUSH

VENTILATION MASK

ELECTRIC DRILL

SCREWDRIVER BIT

PILOT DRILL BIT

COUNTERSINK DRILL BIT

WOOD SCREWS

TAPE MEASURE

PENCIL

TABLE SAW (OPTIONAL)

MATERIALS

5 IDENTICAL EURO BLOCK PALLETS

APPROX 25 PALLET BOARDS

WHITEWASH PAINT (WE USED A WATER-
    BASED WHITE PAINT DILUTED WITH WATER,
    BUT OTHER TECHNIQUES/RECIPES CAN BE
    FOUND ONLINE)

4 HEAVY DUTY INDUSTRIAL CASTORS (2
    LOCKABLE)

01

02

03

04

05

To prepare the pallet boards, please refer to Perfecting your Pallet Boards on page 12.

STRUCTURE:

01 Sand and whitewash four of the pallets using a large brush.

02 Cut the fifth pallet with a hand saw at the outer edge of the middle blocks. This should leave you with a smaller pallet consisting of two blocked ends.

03 Sand and whitewash this pallet in the same way.

04 Take two of the full pallets and slot them back to back (blocks facing out) between the two blocked ends created in step 2. These should sit in between the two ends tightly.

If they don't fit snugly, you can knock one of the blocked ends off on the base pallet and move it until the fit is right, then reattach.

05 With an electric drill, screw the two pallets together through the pallet board frames, piloting and countersinking to avoid cracking. You will need at least four screws across the pallet.

Use the electric drill to pilot, countersink and screw into the blocks at the base of the structure into the centre pallets. Sand, and then screw the next two pallets together in the same way.

06

08

07

06 With help from someone else, lift the two additional pallets onto the structure and position them over the bottom pallets.

07 Screw into the bottom pallets through the top of the blocks. This will require long screws.

08 With someone to help you, lay the entire divider on its side. Attach four castors (one to each corner) to the base of the unit using an electric drill and screws. Place the two lockable castors diagonally opposite each other on the base. Carefully lift the unit back up and make sure the castors are locked in place before you build the shelves.

SHELVES:

You will need 6 identical shelves and 3 bigger ones for the bottom and top. All the shelves are made in the same way, but the measurements will all depend on the size of the pallets used. Before you start, measure the length and width of the shelves on the divider structure: this will determine the measurements needed below.

09 Measure, mark and cut two pallet boards at 100cm (40in) or to the length of the pallets/shelves. You will need a width of approximately 12cm (5in). You may need to use a table saw to cut them to the exact width you require. If you don't have a table saw, you can just leave them as they are and have slightly wider shelves.

Measure, mark and cut three pallet boards at 12cm (5in) or the width of the shelves. Sand all the boards.

10 Place the 12cm (5in) boards at either end of the two 100cm (40in) boards and secure using panel pins, wood glue and a hammer.

11 Measure the remaining gap and divide by 2 to get the centre point. Mark using a pencil.

Measure the 12cm (5in) pallet board widths, divide by 2 and mark the centre.

Align both centre marks and attach to the middle of the shelves.

09

10

11

12

12 Measure, mark and cut a pallet board at 100cm (40in) or to the length of the pallet/shelves. Cut the board down the length using a hand saw or table saw so that you have a width of 3.5cm (1⅜in), or enough to cover the front of the shelves and brace beams. Using a hammer, panel pin nails and wood glue, attach this to the front of the shelves flush with the top to cover the braces underneath.

13 Position the shelves on the pallet blocks and screw them into place.

14 Repeat with all of the shelves, covering the entire surface at the top, and adding front beams to both long edges to finish.

TOP TIP:

For a more cost-effective but less portable room divider, you can make it without the castors and simply sit it on its base.

13

VINTAGE CART

A more advanced project, Billy's vintage cart design uses two different kinds of pallet – the stringer and the two-way entry. The cart relies heavily on chunkier beams (bearers/stringers and notched stringers) with pallet boards used just for the surface. While our version uses cart wheels with metal bracket fixings, a range of wheels can be used and it will all depend on which ones you can source. Try using local online sites or keeping your eyes open at auctions, car boot sales and farm sales or, alternatively, contact your local blacksmith to get them custom-made. Our wheels were very rusty, so we sanded them down, coated them with a primer and sprayed them with a metal paint. Our customers use these carts for potting tables, flower carts, to serve vintage afternoon tea and to dress outdoor summer parties with barbecue food! Please note that while we have endeavoured to describe this project as accurately as possible, measurements may differ depending on your materials. Always measure your project as you work and make adjustments to the instructions as necessary.

TOOLS AND EQUIPMENT

TAPE MEASURE

PENCIL

COMBINATION SQUARE

HAND SAW

ELECTRIC SANDER AND SANDPAPER

VENTILATION MASK

PILOT DRILL BIT

COUNTERSINK DRILL BIT

ELECTRIC DRILL

SCREWDRIVER BIT

HAMMER

WAX CLOTH

MATERIALS

2 HANDLES (NOTCHED STRINGER BEAMS
  FROM A STRINGER OR TWO-WAY ENTRY
  PALLET)

10 PALLET BEARER/STRINGER BEAMS FROM
  TWO-WAY ENTRY PALLETS

CART WHEELS (APPROX 50CM/20IN
  DIAMETER)

30 PALLET BOARDS (APPROX)

WOOD SCREWS AND WASHERS (OPTIONAL)

WOOD GLUE

PANEL PINS (40MM/1½IN)

CLEAR WAX OR DANISH OIL

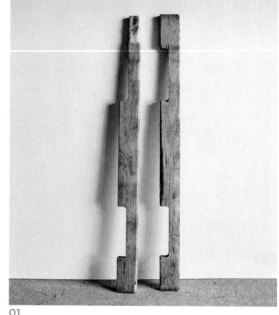

01

To prepare the pallet boards, please refer to Perfecting your Pallet Boards on page 12.

HANDLES:

01 Measure, mark and cut the handles at 120cm (48in) if the handles are too long. Most beams will already be the right size.

02 At one end, mark the beams so they are flush with the notches using a combination square.

03 Cut using a hand saw to create handles.

04 Sand (an electric sander is best here) to round the edges and overall appearance.

BRACE THE HANDLES:

05 Measure and mark a beam at 50cm (20in). Cut using a hand saw. Repeat on a second beam at 44cm (17in), sanding both.

06 Place the first beam (50cm/20in) with the bottom end of the handles flush with each end.

07 Pilot using a drill bit and electric drill. Countersink using an electric drill. Screw into place. The handles should now be attached at the bottom end.

02

03

04

05

06

07

08 From this back beam, measure 73cm (29in) up the handles and mark using a pencil. Place the second beam on the marks. Pilot, countersink and screw as before from the outside edge of the handles so that it sits flush with the top of the frame. This should make the top frame of the cart.

08

BACK LEGS:

09 Measure, mark and cut two beams at 64cm (25in) to create the back legs. Sit each leg into the front notches of the handles on the top frame. From the top of the frame, pilot, countersink and screw the legs into position.

09

10

FRONT LEGS:

10 Measure, mark and cut two uprights at 42cm (16½in). Measure, mark and cut one beam at 35cm (14in). Place the 35cm (14in) beam between the two uprights to make a 'U' shape. Pilot, countersink and screw into position.

11 Sit the frame into the back notch on the handles, now creating an 'n' shape. As with the front legs, pilot, countersink and screw into position from the top of the frame.

11

12

13

WHEELS:

(These steps may differ in measurements and process, depending on the type of wheels you have.)

12 Measure, mark and cut a beam of wood at 50cm (20in). Slot the beam into the metal brackets on the wheels. You may need to knock this in using a hammer and a scrap piece of wood to get a tight fit.

13 Slot the 'n' frame from steps 10 and 11 into the metal wheel bracket structure created in step 12. Pilot and screw from the underside of the metal wheel brackets using long screws so that it attaches through to the n-shaped frame to create back legs. You may need to use washers on the screws.

14 Slot the wheels onto the metal brackets, add the stopper on the end and put a bolt/ pin through the hole: this stops the wheels coming off.

15 Measure, mark and cut the two middle support braces at 63cm (24¾in). Place the support beams just above the metal wheel brackets.

16 Pilot, countersink and screw the beams into place from the back of the back leg. Align the support beam to run square to the front leg. Repeat from the front of the leg to secure into position. These supports will stop the front and back legs bowing inwards.

14

15

16

17

18

19

FRONT LEG CLAD:

17 Measure, mark and cut additional pallet boards at 50.5cm (20in) long. Cut as many as you need to clad the front and back of the 'n' frame legs. Sand the pallet boards. Glue and nail the pallet boards into position until the back legs of the cart are one solid panel. You will need to cut a smaller piece of board to clad between the metal wheel brackets.

TOP CART SURFACE:

18 Measure, mark and cut the pallet boards at 66cm (26in). You will need 13 to 15 boards depending on their width, trimmed (see Perfecting your Pallet Boards on page 12). This gives a nice flush finish. Sand all of the boards front and back. Lay the pallet boards on the top frame to create the cart surface.

19 Glue each board and nail into position using a hammer and pin nails.

20 Once the top surface is complete, measure, mark and cut two pallet boards at 1m (40in) for the trim. Attach to the long edge of the top surface using glue and pin nails. Measure, mark and cut one pallet board at 70cm (27in). Attach to the end of the cart, covering the ends of the long pallet edges. At the handles, measure, mark and cut a pallet board to sit in the centre of the handles and at each end. Attach using pin nails and wood glue.

21 Measure the two small pieces above the handles. Mark and cut a piece of pallet board to fit, attaching as before.

22 Sand the entire cart to finish. Apply a clear wax with a cloth to protect, or varnish if it is to be used outside.

20

21

22

COFFEE TABLE

With furniture too big for our shrinking houses and storage at a minimum, this table is perfect for the space-saving savvy among you. With sleek hair-pin legs and storage concealed with a liftable lid, do you need any more of a reason to add to that ever-growing interior magazine collection? Finished with a white wax, adding a Scandi touch to the hint of industrial metal in the legs, this coffee table is light and non-intrusive for the modern home. Pair it with a scattering of coffee-table books, a well-pruned house plant and a hot mug of coffee, and your guests will be reluctant to leave. For homes with children, increase the length of the pallet bearer beams in step 1 to create a deeper box structure to store toys, arts and crafts or shoes. For the more advanced among you, use a welding machine and reclaimed metal rods (usually found on road work sites) to create your own hair-pin legs like we have here, then finish them with a metal paint or clear lacquer for a more industrial look.

TOOLS AND EQUIPMENT

TAPE MEASURE

PENCIL

COMBINATION SQUARE

TABLE SAW (OPTIONAL)

HAND SAW

ELECTRIC SANDER AND SANDPAPER

VENTILATION MASK

HAMMER

ELECTRIC DRILL OR SCREWDRIVER

WAXING CLOTH OR PAINT BRUSH

MATERIALS

1 PALLET BEARER/STRINGER BEAM

APPROX 30 PALLET BOARDS (DEPENDENT
  ON WIDTHS)

30-40MM (1-1½IN) PANEL PIN NAILS

3 HINGES

WOOD GLUE

20MM WOOD SCREWS

WHITE WAX OR WHITEWASH (WE USE A
  WATER-BASED WHITE PAINT DILUTED WITH
  WATER, BUT OTHER TECHNIQUES/RECIPES
  CAN BE FOUND ONLINE)

4 X HAIR PIN LEGS (CAN BE SOURCED
  ONLINE)

01

*To prepare the pallet boards, please refer to
Perfecting your Pallet Boards on page 12.*

01 Measure, mark and cut four pallet bearer
beams at 16cm (6in) (see Top Tip) to create
the inside support beams. If you have a
table saw, cut two in half down the length on
the saw to create four. We have done this, but
it isn't necessary.

02 Measure, mark and cut 6 pallet boards
at 45cm (18in). Sand the 6 pallet boards and
4 beams.

03 Use three of the pallet boards to clad
two of the support beams by placing one
flush at each end of the pallet boards. Attach
using 30-40mm (1-1½in) panel pin nails, wood
glue and a hammer. You may need to cut
the length of one pallet board to create the
correct width; we do this using a table saw
but a hand saw can be used. Repeat to create
the two end panels of the table.

02

03

04

04 Measure, mark and cut 6 pallet boards at 75cm (30in) and sand. Use these pallet boards to join the two end panels with 30–40mm (1–1½in) panel pin nails, wood glue and a hammer. Again, you may need to trim the excess from the top pallet. This will create the two sides of the table (three pallet boards per side).

TOP TIP:

If you don't have a table saw to trim the boards in step 4, you can begin by cutting the beam to the width of your three pallet boards instead of 16cm (6in).

05

06

07

08

05 Measure, mark and cut an additional 14 pallet boards at 75cm (30in) for the top and bottom of the table. Sand until smooth. Attach the 7 bottom boards with a hammer, panel pins and wood glue to create the main structure.

06 Measure, mark and cut two pallet boards at 43cm (17in). These will brace the top lid of the table. It is always best to check this measurement on your own design by measuring the inside of the main structure. Lay the remainder of the 75cm (30in) pallet boards on a flat surface to create the top panel. You should have a width of 47.5cm (18½in) (or to fit the top of the table).

Measure and mark 7cm (2½in) from both sides and 2cm (¾in) in from the back edge. Clamp together.

07 Lay the two 43cm (17in) pallet boards cut in step 6 onto the inside edge of the marks. Attach using a hammer, panel pins and wood glue to brace the boards together for the top. You should have at least one nail in each pallet board.

08 Place the lid on the box and position the hinges on the back outside edge. Place the first two 5cm (2in) from each edge, and the third in the centre. Screw into place to join the lid to the box.

09

09 Sand the entire table, rounding off pointed corners. Finish the table with a white wax or whitewash. If whitewashing, you may want to add a clear furniture wax to protect the wood and finish.

10 Flip the entire table on its lid. Place the four hair pin legs in each corner and secure with an electric drill and screws (pilot if necessary).

10

TOP TIP:

To make the box deeper, increase the length of the pallet bearer beams in step 1. This will create a larger box, perfect for storing toys.

RECLAIMED FOLDING TABLE

With homes getting smaller, but the need to gather becoming stronger, this fold-away table is perfect for weekend dinner guests and is not only practical but beautiful too. Using simple folding mechanisms sourced online, reclaimed scaffold boards and pallet bearer/stringer beams, this project will cost you considerably less than a table of the same style sourced on the high street. While scaffold boards produce a beautiful aesthetic when sanded, you can adapt the design to suit your interior. There is now a wide range of products on the market to give a coloured wash effect. We love using furniture wax that leaves the grain of the wood visible while adding a hint of colour – a white wax finish gives a great Scandi vibe. Pair the table with the Bench on page 78 to add to the sense of gathering and reduce the need for storing chairs. This project is perfect for the style savvy and not only pulls on visual interior trends but also creates a hygge atmosphere in our homes.

TOOLS AND EQUIPMENT

TAPE MEASURE

COMBINATION SQUARE

PENCIL

HAND SAW

TABLE SAW

ELECTRIC SANDER AND SANDPAPER

VENTILATION MASK

METRE (YARD) RULE

ELECTRIC DRILL

10MM (½IN) DRILL BIT

ELECTRICAL TAPE (OPTIONAL)

ADHESIVE GUN

HAMMER

SCRAP PIECE OF WOOD.

LARGE CLAMPS (APPROX 1½M/3-5FT) – THE
    MORE CLAMPS HERE, THE BETTER

PILOT HOLE DRILL BIT

COUNTERSINK DRILL

SCREWDRIVER BIT

WOOD SCREWS

JIGSAW

OILING CLOTH OR BRUSH

MATERIALS

4 DRY SCAFFOLD BOARDS AT LEAST 180CM
    (6FT) LONG

STRONG WOOD ADHESIVE

5CM (2IN) DOWEL PEGS (APPROX. 20)

6 PALLET BEARER/STRINGER BEAMS
    (AS SQUARE AS POSSIBLE – TRY
    INDUSTRIAL AREAS)

1 LONG PALLET BEARER/STRINGER BEAM
    (180CM/6FT), OR CUT A SCAFFOLD BOARD
    DOWN THE WIDTH ON THE TABLE SAW

4 FOLDING TABLE MECHANISMS
    (2 LOCKABLE)

FINISHING OIL OR DANISH OIL

01

02

'u' grain   'n' grain

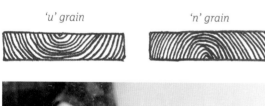

03

To prepare the scaffold boards, please refer to page 11.

STRUCTURE:

01 Mark one end of the scaffold boards using a combination square to ensure you're working from a straight edge. Cut with a hand saw. Measure from the freshly cut edge and mark with a pencil at 180cm (6ft). Cut using a hand saw.

02 Lay out the four boards as the table top. Ensure the end grain of the wood is shaped as a 'u' and not an 'n': this ensures that as the boards move and bow in time, the table doesn't become uneven.

03 Take the two end boards and cut the inside edges on the table saw. (You do not need to remove a lot of material, this is just to give a clean, straight edge.) Only cut the inside edge – this leaves a natural finish to the outer edge that will be seen and ensures the cut edge sits flush with the other boards when assembled.

04 Take the two remaining middle boards, cut down in the same way on both sides using the table saw. You may need assistance holding the board once it is through the table saw. Sand all the boards with an electric sander, wearing a ventiltation mask and working in a well-ventilated room.

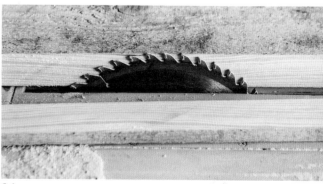

04

05

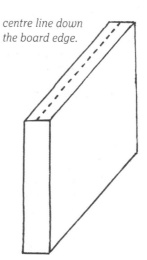

centre line down the board edge.

05 On each cut edge, mark the centre of the board's thickness. Use a metre rule to join the marks, creating a centre line.

On each line, mark every 30cm (1ft). This should now create a cross on the line drawn and give you 5 equal marks.

06 Using an electric drill and a 10mm (½in) drill bit, drill a 2.5cm (1in) hole on each cross mark. We do this by measuring the drill bit and putting tape at the 2.5cm (1in) mark (electrical tape is best) so it's easy to see when you've reached the right depth. Ensure the drill is continuously vertical when drilling the holes to get them straight.

07 Use a good-quality adhesive. Working one board at a time, apply glue to the cut edge and in each hole. Knock the 5cm (2in) dowel pegs into each hole on the first cut edge with a hammer. Continue on every second edge.

08 Knock the boards together using a hammer and a scrap piece of wood. The dowel pegs should slot into the holes on the opposite board.

09 Use the clamps to slowly clamp the boards together until flush. Leave the boards on a flat surface for 2 to 3 days to allow to set.

06

07

08

09

LEGS:

10 Measure, mark and cut the four pallet bearer beams at 70cm (27½in). Measure, mark and cut two pallet bearer beams at 42cm (16½in). Sand all of the beams.

11 Measure and mark 20cm (8in) up from the bottom of each of the longer beams. Place one of the short beams between two of the longer beams onto the marks (the beam sits above the mark). With an electric drill, pilot and countersink two holes into the outside edge of the larger beams and into the centre

beam. Using an electric drill, screw into position. Repeat on the second set.

12 Once the table top is removed from the clamps, flip it over so that it is now on the 'n' grain. Mark 9cm (3½in) in from each end of the table. Place the legs in position so that the outside edge of the leg is flush with the 9cm (3½in) mark.

13 Using an electric drill, screw the folding mechanism into the inside (at the top) of each one of the legs. The folding mechanisms will consist of two lockable and two folding

10

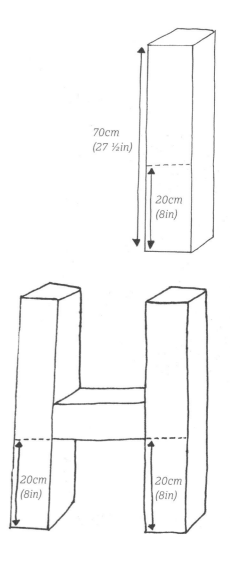

70cm
(27 ½in)

20cm
(8in)

20cm
(8in)

20cm
(8in)

11

systems. Ensure that the two lockable systems sit diagonally opposite each other on the two sets of legs. Screw the other side of the folding table mechanism into the table top.

14 Measure from the outer base of the two legs and add 13cm (5in) onto the final measurement. Measure, mark and cut the longer pallet bearer/stringer beam. Measure 6.5cm (2½in) in from each end of the beam.

12

13

14

15 Measure the centre beam on the table legs.

16 Using a combination square, tape measure and ruler, mark a rectangle the same width as the centre leg beam from the 6.5cm (2½in) marks. Mark halfway up the width of the beam. This will create a slot to sit over the legs in order to support them and stop them from folding in when the table is in use.

17 Measure the centre beam on the table legs. Cut down both vertical sides of the rectangle

15

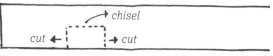

16

17

using a hand saw. Knock the remainder out using a hammer and a chisel.

18 Sand the beam. Slot the beam over the centre supports of the legs to stop them from folding in.

19 Sand the entire table, rounding off corners and edges.

20 Coat with a finishing oil to protect.

TOP TIP:

If you do not want to use the folding leg systems, simply screw the legs into position from the top of the table surface and dowel the countersink to neaten and finish (see page 15).

18

19

20

BENCH

The perfect accessory to the reclaimed folding table, this bench is great for seating additional weekend guests. With the versatility of the bench, you may find you never want to fold it down. Whether it is used in the hall, kids' room or garden, it's great for adaptable seating. In the workshop, we've had a huge amount of table and bench commissions as extended families get larger and time spent together gets more important. The benches are also used regularly in our prop hire as they can be easily moved from ceremonies to receptions, saving space and money on the big day. For family homes with children, try adding typography with wood-burning pyrography techniques or vinyl application to add the children's names to show where they sit at mealtimes.

TOOLS AND EQUIPMENT

TAPE MEASURE

PENCIL

COMBINATION SQUARE

HAND SAW OR ELECTRIC MITRE SAW

TABLE SAW OR CIRCULAR SAW

ELECTRIC SANDER AND SANDPAPER

VENTILATION MASK

PILOT HOLE DRILL BIT

COUNTERSINK DRILL BIT

ELECTRIC DRILL

SCREWDRIVER BIT

PAINT BRUSH OR OILING CLOTH

MATERIALS

2 SCAFFOLD BOARDS APPROX. 180CM (6FT)
   LONG (YOU WILL USE 1.5 OF THESE)

SCAFFOLD BOARD OFFCUTS OR BOARD AT
   LEAST 35CM (14IN) LONG

LARGE WOOD SCREWS

30MM (1IN) WOOD SCREWS

2 INDUSTRIAL PALLET BEARER BEAMS
   APPROX. 200CM (6FT 5IN) – WE SOURCE
   THESE FROM INDUSTRIAL SITES AS THEY'RE
   MORE SQUARE THAN USUAL PALLETS

4 FOLDING LEG SYSTEMS (2 LOCKABLE)

DANISH OIL

01

02

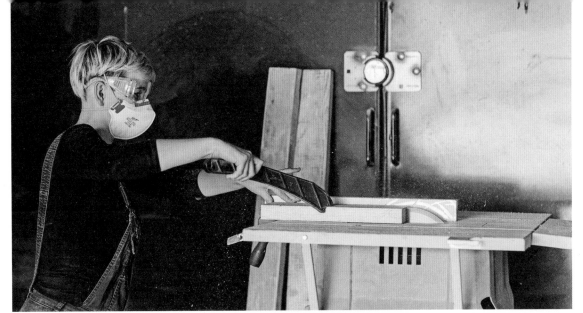

03

To prepare the scaffold boards, please refer to page 11.

01 Measure the two scaffold boards at 170cm (5½ft), mark with a pencil and a combination square. As with pallet boards, we always trim the end we measure from to ensure a straight cut. Cut using a hand saw or mitre saw.

02 Using a table saw or circular saw, cut these scaffold boards into three 10cm (4in) wide lengths. You will be left with a 2cm (¾in) wide offcut from one of the boards – keep this for use later on (see step 13).

04

03 Cut a piece of scaffold board at 35cm (14in) long. Using the table saw, cut two 5cm (2in) wide pieces from the 35cm (14in) board. This will create the two end beams to brace the boards on the bench seat.

04 Sand all of the boards from the above steps. It is best to use an electric sander with scaffold boards. Lay the three 170cm (5½ft) x 10cm (4in) boards on the 'U' grain.

05 Place the two 35cm (14in) x 5cm (2in) beams at each end so that the two outer centre boards are flush with the end edges. Ensure the centre board is positioned centrally between them.

05

06

07

08

09

06 Mark the placement of the boards onto the ends so you can see where to pilot.

07 Use an electric drill, pilot hole, countersink, screwdriver bit and screws to secure the two side centre boards flush with the end beams. Repeat this at both ends. If you would like to cover the screws with dowel to neaten them, see page 15 for instructions.

08 Measure, mark and cut four industrial bearer beams at 40cm (16in), and two industrial bearer beams at 15cm (6in). Sand all the beams until smooth.

Measure 15cm (6in) up from the bottom of two of the 40cm (16in) beams, mark using a pencil and combination square.

09 Place a 15cm (6in) beam in the centre of the 40cm (16in) beams in line with the marks created above. This should create a 'H' shape. It may be easier to clamp once in position to secure for the next step.

10

10 From the outside edge of the 40cm (16in) beam, pilot and countersink two holes in each side using an electric drill. Using an electric drill, screwdriver bit and screws, attach the centre beam to the two outside beams. Repeat with the remaining three beams. This will create the leg structures.

11 Place the two leg structures at each end of the underside of the bench. These should sit flush with the inside edge of the end brace beams on the bench. Place the folding leg systems centrally on the inside of the legs. Make sure the lock is placed on the outside edge so that it is accessible and that the locking mechanisms are diagonally opposite each other on the bench.

12 Attach the folding leg systems to the underside of the bench using wood screws and an electric drill. Secure the folding systems to the inside edge of the legs to secure and join to the bench.

11

12

13

13 Sand the 170cm (¾in x 5½ft) scaffold board offcut from step 3 as a support between the two legs. Screw this in to avoid the legs folding in while in use – this can be done with a screwdriver once piloted.

14 Give the entire bench a final sand to smooth all joins.

15 Coat the bench with Danish Oil to protect against everyday use.

14

15

TOP TIPS:

If you prefer, you can create a slotting support for the bench – just follow the instructions for the table slotting support on page 74.

If you don't want to use the folding leg systems, simply screw the legs into position from the top of the bench seat surface and dowel the countersink to neaten and finish.

You can use regular pallet bearer beams if you can't source industrial ones, but the measurements will need to be adjusted.

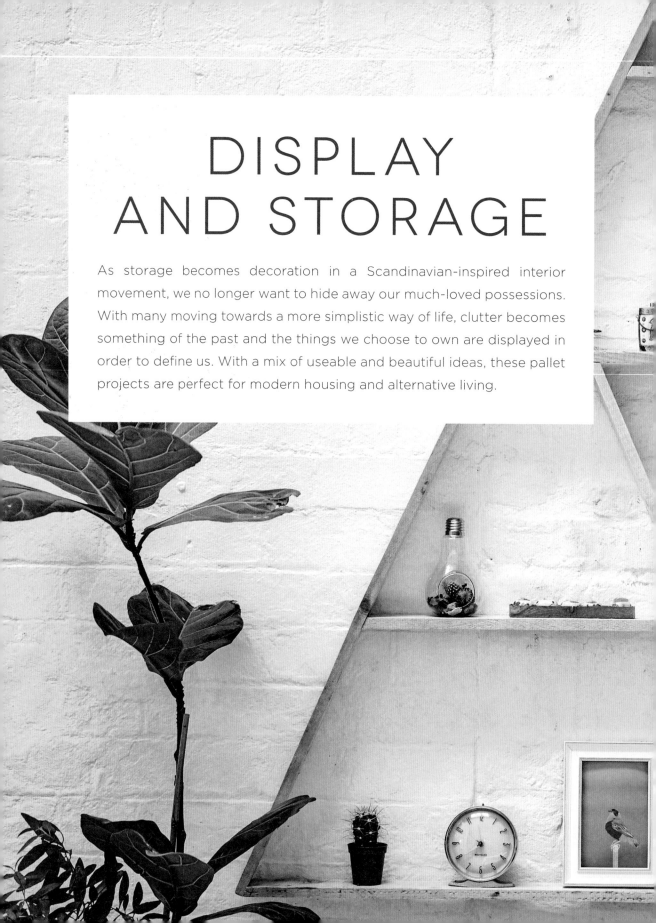

DISPLAY
AND STORAGE

As storage becomes decoration in a Scandinavian-inspired interior movement, we no longer want to hide away our much-loved possessions. With many moving towards a more simplistic way of life, clutter becomes something of the past and the things we choose to own are displayed in order to define us. With a mix of useable and beautiful ideas, these pallet projects are perfect for modern housing and alternative living.

TOWEL RAIL

With the modern ability to add style to every element of our homes, gone are the days of hiding towels and throws in cupboards and drawers. With houses becoming smaller and storage a thing of the past, we crave practical and stylish solutions for displaying the things we love. This simple design adds natural style and chic to a bathroom (or bedroom), giving your guests a sense of luxury when washing their hands. This design fits to a range of spaces – I even stored towels on one of these quirky ladders in our tiny boat. Made purely from pallets and an old broom handle, this can be reinvented as you wish. Add more shelves to hold rolled or folded clean towels or for soaps and candles – it's easy to adapt to your personal needs.

———

TOOLS AND EQUIPMENT

TAPE MEASURE

COMBINATION SQUARE

PENCIL

HAND SAW/ELECTRIC CHOP/MITRE SAW

CLAMPS

FLAT DRILL BIT (DIAMETER OF YOUR RAILS)

ELECTRIC SANDER AND SANDPAPER

VENTILATION MASK

HAMMER

SCRAP WOOD

CLAMPS (OPTIONAL)

ELECTRIC DRILL

HOLE SAW TO SUIT YOUR POT (OURS IS 89MM
   (3½IN) – MEASURE BELOW THE POT LIP FOR
   APPROXIMATE DIMENSION)

PILOT DRILL BIT (TO SUIT SCREWS)

COUNTERSINK DRILL BIT (10MM/½IN DIAMETER)

SCREWDRIVER DRILL BIT (TO SUIT SCREWS)

9MM (½IN) DOWEL

WAX CLOTH

MATERIALS

2 THICK PALLET SUPPORT BEAMS (OR SIMILAR)

OLD BROOM HANDLE OR THICK DOWEL
   (25–30MM/1IN)

2 PALLET WOOD BOARDS (APPROX)

PANEL PIN NAILS (30–40MM/1–1½IN)

WOOD GLUE

WOOD SCREWS

WHITE WAX

PLANT POT

*To prepare the pallet boards, please refer to
Perfecting your Pallet Boards on page 12.*

01 Measure the two chunky legs/uprights at
120cm (48in). Mark with a combination square
and a pencil, and cut with a hand saw.
Now measure 30cm (1ft) from the top and
bottom of both uprights and then 2 x 17.5cm
(7in) from the bottom mark. This will give four
marks. You should end up with a gap of 25cm
(10in) between the 3rd and top mark.

02 Measure the depth of the upright and
make the original mark into a cross to centre
on the uprights.

03 Clamp the uprights onto a flat surface.
Using a flat drill bit (the same width as your
dowel diameter), drill out all of the holes
by centring the flat drill bit on the marked
crosses. Drill at least 3cm (1in) deep (judge
this depth on the upright size). Sand both of
the legs including the drilled holes.

04 Measure the broom handle at 35cm (14in).
Cut with a hand saw to make the rails. It may
be easier to clamp the broom handle here
for ease of cutting. Sand with a high-grit
sandpaper by hand.

TOP TIP:

*Tape the flat drill bit with electrical tape to
define the depth you wish to drill.*

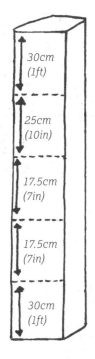

01

02

03

04

05

06

07

05 Lay the uprights on a flat surface (holes facing upwards). Dip one end of the rail into wood glue and knock into the drilled hole. Continue with all of the rails.

06 Glue the other end of the rails and knock the second upright onto the rails. You may need to use a hammer and a scrap piece of wood to avoid damaging the uprights. If you have some bigger clamps, you could clamp the rail at this stage to keep it tight in place until the glue dries.

07 Measure the gap at the top of the ladder for your shelf width. Deduct 3cm (1in) from this measurement to allow for the pallet side supports. For example, overall gap width 40 – 3 = 37cm (16 – 1 = 15in) shelf width.

08 Measure and cut the shelf at the required width with a tape measure, combination square and hand saw. Decide where you'd like the hole for the pot support and measure into the centre of the shelf creating a cross as in step 2.

08

09

10

09 Clamp the shelf and drill out the hole using an appropriately sized hole saw and electric drill, centred onto your marked cross. Sand the shelf and inside the cut hole.

10 Measure an appropriate height for the side shelf pallet (we would recommend at least 10cm/4in) and cut two pieces using a hand saw and combination square. You can cut the width of the pallet boards here to sit within the width of the uprights if necessary. Sand and nail the two side shelf pallets either side of the shelf using glue and panel pins. Ensure the bottom of the side shelf is flush with the bottom of the shelf.

TOP TIP:

Define the hole saw size by measuring the diameter under the lip of the plant pot.

12

11

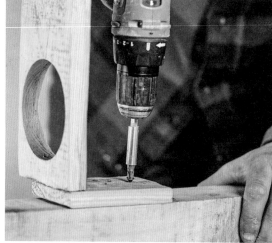

13

11 Using an electric drill, pilot both the side pallets using an appropriate drill bit at the bottom of the 30cm mark made in step 1.

12 Add a deep countersink of at least 10mm (4in) diameter by 5mm (⅜in) depth.

13 Screw the shelf onto the inside of the ladder uprights.

14 Dip the dowel into the glue and knock into the 5mm (⅜in) countersink.

15 Cut the dowel close to the ladder upright surface with a hand saw.

16 Leave to dry and sand off the excess dowel.

17 Wax using a white wax and wax cloth.

14

15

16

17

DISPLAY SHELF

This project is great for beginners through to experts thanks to the variety of designs and uses for which it can be adapted. One of our bestselling pieces, I've seen these shelves used in children's rooms, as spice racks, memory walls or simply for displaying trinkets that are too nice to be kept in a drawer. With Scandi-inspired embellishment, this project is perfect if you want to personalise to match your colour scheme or interior. Try different size variations to create outdoor planters, bookshelves or window gardens. This design is one you could make several times to suit its use throughout the home. For easier versions, try straight pallet backs rather than the uneven back we have here, or add a shelf at the bottom to make it freestanding. For more advanced levels, incorporate angled cuts along the top to add a different dimension to the overall shape. Play with incorporating the pot holder used on the towel rail on page 93 to hold terracotta pots of succulents or stationery. This design encourages you to think outside the box, so have a little fun with it and enjoy!

TOOLS AND EQUIPMENT

TAPE MEASURE

COMBINATION SQUARE

PENCIL

HAND SAW OR ELECTRIC CHOP/MITRE SAW

ELECTRIC SANDER AND SANDPAPER

VENTILATION MASK

HAMMER

METRE (YARD) RULE

GOOD-QUALITY MASKING TAPE

SMALL PAINT BRUSH

COTTON BUD (OPTIONAL)

MATERIALS

PALLET WOOD

WOOD GLUE

PANEL PINS (30-40MM/1-1½IN)

CLEAR VARNISH (OPTIONAL)

PICTURE HOOK PLATES

CHALK PAINT

01

To prepare the pallet boards, please refer to Perfecting your Pallet Boards on page 12.

01 Measure the back pallet boards to a length of 44cm (17in) and mark using a combination square and a pencil. Cut the back panel boards using a hand saw. Continue until you have enough for a width of approx. 40cm (16in) for the shelf. Sand all the back panel boards using sandpaper or an electric sander.

02

03

04

02 Repeat for the shelf pallet boards, measuring at 40cm (16in) and marking with a combination square. Consider what you'd like to put on your shelves as this will determine the width of pallet board required. Cut the shelf pallets with a hand saw and sand.

03 Lay the back panels out on a flat surface in your preferred design. Lay the bottom shelf in place and align by eye, then run a pencil along the bottom edge. Remove the bottom shelf and use a combination square to adjust the drawn line until straight. Place the shelf back in position.

04 Place the second shelf onto the back panels and measure between the two shelves to ensure this is also straight. Mark the second shelf along the bottom edge using a pencil.

05

06

07

08

TOP TIP:

Add picture hook plates to the top of the shelf to secure to the wall.

05 Continue the lines onto the sides of the end back panels using a pencil and a combination square. This is so the markings will be visible from the back. Number the back panels at the top and flip the boards over so that the back is now facing upwards.

06 Sit the two shelves under the two end back panels, using the second shelf as support, then match the first end panel with the bottom of the shelf using with the side markings made in step 5. Glue and tack the first shelf into position using panel pins and a hammer, allowing at least two panel pins for each back panel.

07 Repeat with the second end panel to create the main structure of the shelf. Attach the second shelf in the same way, aligning the bottom of the shelf with the side markings on both end panels.

08 Lay the remainder of the back panels onto the shelves, lining up the markings made on the front with the bottom of each shelf. Using a metre rule, join the side markings with a pencil to create a line along the back – this will create a guide for nailing. Nail the remainder of the backboards into position. Sand the entire shelf to ensure a smooth finish.

09 Mask the geometric shapes using good-quality masking tape. Paint with a small paint brush. Create the dot design using the small brush or cotton bud.

09

OVER-BED SHELVES

A beautiful accessory to the platform bed, this project is great for the trinket lovers, collectors and foragers – for those, like me, who love nothing more than displaying jars of buttons, stones, sands, rocks, maps and books. It's made entirely from pallet wood, but we have added a contemporary edge with the addition of geometrics, a particular love of mine. By playing with the shapes, you can create spaces and compartments personal to your needs and possessions. Don't be put off by the angled cuts as we have great hints and tips on how to make this super simple to achieve, and suited to all abilities. Translate the design into different areas of your home by increasing the size to make library wall shelves or dresser tops. We love this and will soon be adding one to our collection!

TOOLS AND EQUIPMENT

TAPE MEASURE

PENCIL

MITRE SAW OR HAND SAW

ELECTRIC SANDER AND SANDPAPER

VENTILATION MASK

LIGHT-DUTY NAIL GUN (OR PANEL PINS)

HAMMER

MATERIALS

3 PALLET BOARDS 2-3M (6½-10FT) LONG

8 PALLET BOARDS UP TO 2M (6½FT) LONG

WOOD GLUE

THIN PANEL PINS

01

To prepare the pallet boards, please refer to Perfecting your Pallet Boards on page 12.

01 Measure, mark and straight cut 3 pallet boards (1 x 180cm/6ft, 2 x 200cm/6½ft) with a hand saw or mitre saw. Place the boards in a triangular shape with the 180cm (6ft) board at the base.

02 Sit the two side boards over the top of the base corners and draw a line underneath to create a guide for the angle needed.

03 Cut the angles using a mitre saw or hand saw. Repeat at the top with one of the pallet boards placed onto the second. Cut the board with a mitre saw or hand saw.

04 Sand the three pallet boards.

05 Secure the wood into the triangle using wood glue and a nail gun or thin panel pins.

02

03

04

05

06 Measure from the top point down the triangle on both sides and make marks at 40cm (16in), 80cm (32in), 120cm (4ft) and 160cm (5¼ft). This is to mark where the shelves will go.

07 For each shelf, place a pallet board on top of the frame at the marks, and use a pencil to mark the angle underneath as you did in step 2. Cut the angles using a mitre saw or hand saw.

08 Attach the shelves at each mark using wood glue, a nail gun or small panel pins.

09 Using the same technique, create and secure the vertical sections. To fix, use picture frame fixings or L brackets.

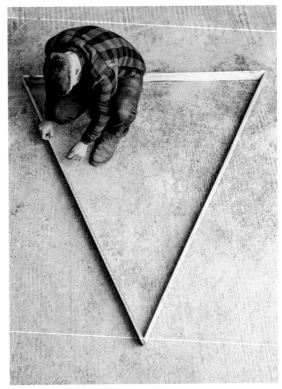

06

07

08

09

HERB BOX PLANTER

Using reclaimed leather offcuts from our local leather supplier (you can also use old leather belts), this is a simple and quick project to use up parts of a pallet you would usually discard. Made with basic tools and materials, this finished piece looks effective and is really versatile around the house. It's great for herbs, storage, or toiletries in the bathroom – you can adapt the design to suit your needs. Try replacing the colour wash with elements of chalkboard paint so you can personalise with labels, comments or quotes, or try using upcycled cupboard handles treated for outdoor use. This project is perfect for small window or balcony gardens, or, if you have a larger space, attached under shed windows to add quaint decoration to otherwise unused space. Experiment with your plants, growing herbs for cooking or botanicals for adding to homemade gin and cocktails in the summer – a personal touch that's sure to impress your guests on those long, warm evenings.

TOOLS AND EQUIPMENT

TAPE MEASURE

COMBINATION SQUARE

PENCIL

HAND SAW

TABLE SAW (OPTIONAL)

ELECTRIC SANDER AND SANDPAPER

VENTILATION MASK

HAMMER

WAX CLOTH

SCISSORS

STAPLE GUN AND STAPLES

STANLEY (UTILITY) KNIFE/FABRIC SCISSORS

CUTTING BOARD

METAL RULE

MATERIALS

PALLET BLOCKED END FROM A EURO PALLET

2-3 PALLET BOARDS

WOOD GLUE

ROUND WIRE NAILS APPROX. 40-50MM
  (1½-2IN)

COLOURWASH PAINT OR COLOURED WAX

CLEAR VARNISH (FOR OUTDOOR PLANTER)

PLANT LINER OR RUBBLE SACKS

LEATHER OFFCUTS/METAL HANDLES (FOR
  OUTDOOR PLANTER)

4 GALVANISED CLOUT NAILS APPROX. 40MM
  (1½IN)

01

Decide on the size you'd like your planter. For this project, this is determined by the size of your pallet end and where your blocks are. If you would like to use the whole end, steps 1 and 2 aren't necessary. Ours is two blocks wide. To prepare the pallet boards, please refer to Perfecting your Pallet Boards on page 12, but in this case do not trim the ends of the pallet blocks before beginning.

01 Mark to the end of the second block from the end of the pallet with a pencil and combination square.

02 Use a hand saw to cut and remove the unwanted material.

03 You should now have two sides and two ends. Measure the bottom of the planter to create the base using a tape measure.

04 Mark and cut the pallet wood to fit using a hand saw. Depending on the planter's width, you may have to use two pieces of pallet wood and you may have to cut one of these down the length of the board – we use a table saw. If you don't have the tools to do this, leave the pallet piece whole to act as a lip on the front

02

03

04

05

of the planter, ensuring the back board is flush to the side. Sand the bottom pallet boards and attach to the planter using wood glue, round wire nails and a hammer. Knock into the blocks at the ends of the planter.

05 Sand the entire planter, rounding off the corners where needed.

06 Using a coloured wax and a cloth, apply wax to the planter and wait for it to dry. You can wax on the inside if you wish, but this isn't necessary as it will be lined. However, if you plan to use the planter outside, it is always best to varnish the inside before lining.

06

07

08

09

10

07 Lay the liner inside the planter leaving excess at the top. Cut the liner slightly bigger than needed using scissors.

08 Fold down the edges of the liner flush with the top of the planter and staple into place with a staple gun.

09 Measure the ends of the planter (at the blocks) add 6cm (2½in) onto this measurement to establish the length of the leather handle needed.

10 Cut the leather using a Stanley knife (on a cutting board) or fabric scissors (depending on thickness) and a metal ruler, rounding the two ends. Cut approximately 3.5cm (1¼in) wide. Attach the leather handles using the galvanised clout nails (one in each end), dipping them into wood glue before hammering into place. Be sure to allow excess leather in the centre of your handle in order to enable carrying.

If your planter is for outside use, metal handles will be more appropriate and a few coats of clear varnish over the wood are always recommended.

TOP TIP:

If you're using the planter outside for bedded plants, use an electric drill with a 10mm drill bit to drill several holes through the liner and the bottom of the planter for drainage.

RECYCLING CENTRE

What better way to glam up your recycling than by upcycling a cupboard to store it all? This is the perfect project for utility areas and kitchens and makes way for the ever-growing demand to recycle household waste. With the population becoming more knowledgeable about sustainability, we are even more motivated in our studio to save as much as we can from landfill. While working with pallets and other salvaged woods reduces a huge amount of industrial waste, we also push for sustainability in other areas of our business. We currently work with other small independent local businesses to recycle their cardboard packaging, creating our own boxes from waste to send out our goods to stockists and online customers. We are also huge fans of car boot sales, auctions and charity stores, where we source a lot of our fabrics, trims, tools and furniture. Sustainability and recycling can be daunting and time consuming, so find ways to make it fun in your household. For us, recycling has become a hobby and a business and there is nothing more thrilling for us than finding a real treasure in someone else's castoffs.

———

TOOLS AND EQUIPMENT

TAPE MEASURE

COMBINATION SQUARE

PENCIL

HAND SAW

SAND PAPER AND/OR ELECTRIC SANDER

VENTILATION MASK

PILOT HOLE

COUNTERSINK DRILL BIT

ELECTRIC DRILL

SCREWDRIVER BIT

127MM (5IN) HOLE SAW

DAMP CLOTH

PAINT BRUSHES

GOOD-QUALITY MASKING TAPE

WAX CLOTH OR BRUSH

MATERIALS

OLD CUPBOARD

20 PALLET BOARDS

PANEL PINS

CHALK/FURNITURE PAINT

CHALKBOARD PAINT

CLEAR FURNITURE WAX

01

To prepare the pallet boards, please refer to Perfecting your Pallet Boards on page 12.

01 Measure, mark and cut 12 pieces (6 each side) of pallet board at 75.5cm (30in) or to fit the side of your cupboard. Sand the board. Position in place and attach the boards to the outside of the cabinet using pin nails and a hammer. (See TOP TIP.)

02

02 Repeat for the top of the cabinet, measuring and cutting the wood to fit. Secure in the same way as step 1.

03 Sand all the pallet wood using an electric sander.

TOP TIP:

If the wood of your cabinet is quite thin and the nails come through on the inside, line the inside of your cabinet with a piece of plywood cut to size or screw the pallet boards from the inside of the cupboard.

03

04

04 Measure the containers you are using inside your cabinet. Measure the diameter of the hole saw and halve it. Add these two figures together.

05 Measure and mark this distance from the bottom of the doors. Measure the width of the cupboard doors and mark the centre of each, creating a cross on the previous marks.

06 Using the hole saw and an electric drill, drill the hole into the doors centring the middle of the hole saw on the marked cross.

07 Sand the remainder of the cupboard by hand, creating a key/score for painting. Be sure to get in the hole to neaten the cut. Wipe the wood work clean.

08 Paint the trim and doors of the cupboard, leave to dry and apply a second coat if necessary.

09 Mark a square onto each of the doors using masking tape. Paint with chalkboard paint. When it's dry, you can use these for signs to personalise the recycling content. Wax the entire cupboard to protect the pallet boards and paintwork.

05

06

07

09

LOG STORAGE

What better way to embrace a sense of hygge in the home than to have a stack of logs adding warmth and cosiness. Based on one of our previous designs, this project is both practical and beautiful. With the crate-like style, not only does it sit with trends that encourage storage as decoration, it also doubles up as a spare seat for those extended family dinners. With industrial style castors adding a cool touch, it is also transportable from room to room, indoors to outdoors. This design is a great one to learn as it is based on a basic crate structure that my stepdad taught me one Sunday afternoon in his garage some years ago. It includes basic making skills which I have continued to transfer into lots of our projects. Try repeating the design, stacking and attaching crates with castors on the bottom, making moveable book shelves and versatile storage.

———

TOOLS AND EQUIPMENT

TAPE MEASURE

PENCIL

COMBINATION SQUARE

HAND SAW

TABLE SAW (OPTIONAL)

ELECTRIC SANDER AND SANDPAPER

VENTILATION MASK

HAMMER

SCRAP PIECE OF PALLET BOARD OR SPACER

PAINT BRUSH OR WAX CLOTH

ELECTRIC DRILL

DRILL BIT

SCREWDRIVER BIT

WOOD SCREWS

MATERIALS

THICK PALLET BOARDS OR SUPPORT BEAMS
(4 OR 2 DEPENDING ON HOW YOU USE
THEM – SEE STEP 2)

35 PALLET BOARDS (SIMILAR THICKNESS)

WOOD GLUE

PANEL PINS (30MM/1IN)

WAX OR WASH PAINT

4 CASTORS (2 X LOCKABLE)

01

To prepare the pallet boards, please refer to Perfecting your Pallet Boards on page 12.

01 Measure the thicker, beam pallet wood at 45cm (18in) long with a tape measure, pencil and combination square. Repeat this so you have two pieces.

02 Cut the pallets using a hand saw. We cut our pallet pieces in half down the length on a table saw in order to create four thinner, beam-like pieces. However, this is not essential and if you don't have a table saw, cut four of the thicker pallet boards in step 1 rather than the two suggested.

03 Measure the side pallet boards at 40cm (16in). Cut the side pallet boards using a hand saw. Sand the boards.

02

03

04

04 Using two of the support beams from steps 1 and 2, attach the 40cm (16in) side pallet boards to the beams at each end using wood glue, panel pin nails and a hammer. Always attach the top and bottom boards first in order to create the shape and size panel you need.

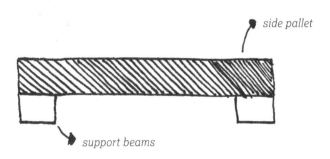

side pallet

support beams

05

06

07

08

05 Space the boards evenly – we do this using a scrap piece of pallet wood to sit in between each board while we attach it. To ensure the boards fit perfectly and to avoid cutting them down the length, space the boards by eye. Attach them as you did the top and bottom pieces in step 4. Repeat to create two identical side panels using the remaining support beams from steps 1 and 2.

06 In the same way that you cut the side panels, cut the top and bottom boards at 50cm (20in) by measuring, marking and cutting with a hand saw. Take the two side panels from step 5 and connect using the top and bottom boards with wood glue, panel pins and a hammer, matching up with the pallet boards on the side panels.

07 Complete one side at a time by attaching the end of the 50cm (20in) boards to each panel side. As before, attach the top and bottom boards first to hold the shape, spacing the boards appropriately in between to match the side panels. Once both sides are complete you should have the basic crate structure.

08 Measure and cut the back boards in the same way at 50cm (20in) and attach to the back of the crate, which should now complete the main structure. Sand the entire crate.

09 Use a paintbrush to apply the colour wash to the crate inside and out. Leave to dry.

10 Turn the crate so that you can work on the bottom. Place the four castors in each corner, with the two lockable castors positioned diagonally opposite each other. Using an electric drill and a small drill bit, pilot the castor screw holes into the pallet board and beams. Use the electric drill and appropriate drill bit and screw the castors into each corner.

09

10

ACCESSORIES

Through my love of interiors, accessorising has always been a more sustainable and affordable way of switching up the look and feel of a room without the need to change every component. The pallet projects in the following chapter are both fun and versatile, allowing you to personalise your space to really reflect you. With something for most elements of the home, these projects take more of a crafty twist, making them a great starting point in preparation for some of the bigger projects.

FOOD TRAY

For those lazy Sunday mornings or Friday evening gatherings, at Nikkita Palmer Designs we continuously use our food trays. This project promotes a sense of hygge around the table, in front of a film or in the garden, indulging a love for gathering, feasting and exploring new foods among friends and family. From winter to summer, housing soups, biscuits, refreshments and cheeses, you really won't believe how useful these boards are until you have one. Using simple techniques and basic tools and materials, these boards also make great gifts, especially when paired with cheese and antipasti selections. For more advanced, crafty designs, use pyrography to personalise, burning initials, quotes or sayings into the boards. For additional uses, adapt the measurements, make a board long enough to fit across the bath to house wine, candles and a book for those long relaxing soaks. Replace the handles with recycled metal cupboard handles or rope for a nautical feel.

———

TOOLS AND EQUIPMENT

TAPE MEASURE

COMBINATION SQUARE

PENCIL

HAND SAW OR ELECTRIC CHOP/MITRE SAW

ELECTRIC SANDER AND SANDPAPER

VENTILATION MASK

HAMMER

STANLEY (UTILITY) KNIFE

CUTTING BOARD

WAX CLOTH

MATERIALS

6 PALLET BOARDS

30MM (1IN) PANEL PINS

WOOD GLUE

LEATHER - OLD BELTS, HORSE BRIDLES OR
  OFFCUTS

25-30MM (1IN) GALVANISED CLOUT NAILS

FOOD-SAFE WAX OR FINISH

To prepare the pallet boards, please refer to Perfecting your Pallet Boards on page 12.

01 Measure and mark (with a combination square and tape measure) four pallet boards at 60cm (24in). When placed together, ours came to a width of 22cm (8½in). Cut the boards using a hand saw and sand until smooth.

02 Measure and cut two pallet boards at 22cm (8½in) (or the width of your boards) and sand. Lay the two short boards on a flat surface vertically, laying the 60cm (24in) boards on top horizontally with the ends flush with the short boards.

03 Use a hammer, panel pins and wood glue to attach the vertical and horizontal boards from the underside of the tray (horizontal boards facing upwards).

04 Flip the board so it is the correct way up. Sand the entire board to finish.

05 Measure the leather at 23cm (9in). Cut using a Stanley (utility) knife and cutting board. Attach one end of the leather in the centre of the vertical supports using the clout nails and a hammer so that it is flush with the edge of the boards. Attach the opposite end, making it flush with the vertical board edge. This should create a handle in the centre large enough to enable carrying. Repeat for the second handle. Apply a food-safe wax with a cloth..

01

02

03

04

05

WALL HANGING

This incredibly simple design is perfect for displaying artwork, wall hangings or throws. Made using a thin strip of pallet wood, rope and hand-painted designs, it looks really effective in little time. While we have used a thin pallet board, a wider board can be cut down on a table saw or used whole for a chunkier effect. If you would like to recreate our knitted wall hanging, this design is perfect for those of you who love to recycle. It was made using old T-shirts, cut into strips and knitted using oversized knitting needles. While larger needles have been popular recently and can be sourced online, why not make your own using an old broom handle, sanding the points at one end and attaching wood to the opposite end as a stopper. Alternatively, use a tree branch – cobnut tree branches are great for this as they're very straight. These needles are also a great display piece, propped in a corner or hung from the wall.

TOOLS AND EQUIPMENT

TAPE MEASURE

PENCIL

HAND SAW

ELECTRIC DRILL

10MM (½IN) DRILL BIT

ELECTRIC SANDER AND SANDPAPER

VENTILATION MASK

SMALL PAINT BRUSH

WAX CLOTH OR BRUSH

FABRIC SCISSORS

MATERIALS

1 PALLET BOARD

WHITE CHALK PAINT

CLEAR FURNITURE WAX

10MM (½IN) THICK JUTE ROPE (ABOUT 2M
   (6½FT LONG)

ASSORTMENT OF OLD GREY, WHITE AND
   CREAM T-SHIRTS

01

To prepare the pallet boards, please refer to Perfecting your Pallet Boards on page 12.

01 Measure the pallet board – ours was 110cm (43in) using a tape measure. Many pallet boards will already be an appropriate length, but if necessary, mark and cut to your chosen length with a hand saw. Measure 4.5cm (1¾in) in from each end and mark (on the side) using a pencil. Using an electric drill, drill through the pallet board on the marks with a 10mm/1cm (½in) drill bit.

02 Sand the pallet board and any rough areas on the holes. Use a small paint brush and a white chalk paint to paint the design onto the board. Leave to dry.

03 Wax using a clear furniture wax.

02

03

04

04 Measure 180cm (6ft) of rope. Cut using fabric scissors. Thread each end of the rope through the holes in the pallet board. Knot each end to stop it slipping back through.

05

06

CREATING YARN FOR KNITTING

05 Lay your T-shirts on a clean, flat surface. Cut up both side seams and across the top seam to give two separate T-shirt sides. I also removed the sleeves to give an easier shape to work with.

06 Cut your fabric into a long strip using good-quality fabric scissors – it is best to do this in a zig-zag shape, as shown, to give a continuous piece of fabric when knitting.

07 Attach your fabric strips together by knotting at the ends and trimming the excess.

08 Wrap the yarn into a ball.

09 Knit your wall hanging using large knitting needles and the T-shirt yarn (you can find knitting tutorials online). When you're finished, drape it over the pallet bar.

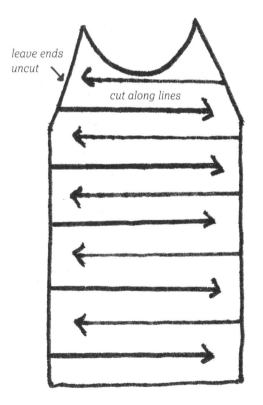

leave ends uncut

cut along lines

07

08

09

CHALKBOARD FRAME

Using an old cupboard door, pallet boards and wine corks, this is the ultimate recycling project. Gone are the days of scraps of paper on the fridge! Perfect for a family home, this chalk- and pinboard is great for simple reminders, uplifting quotes, postcards and kids' creations, and with an element of colour, this project is easily adapted to your space. While not only on trend, cork is also very sustainable. Coming from a cork oak tree, it can be harvested every seven to ten years by extracting the bark from the trunk, therefore unlike other woods in the industry, the tree does not need to be cut down to produce the material. The cork will then regrow, making it a renewable resource. The cork oak is cultivated in Portugal and can also be found in Spain, Morocco and Italy. Cork is now very popular in the fashion industry, with cork fabrics, as well as in interior design, with entire cork walls making an appearance in interactive offices and tactile environments.

TOOLS AND EQUIPMENT

TAPE MEASURE

PENCIL

COMBINATION SQUARE

HAND SAW

ELECTRIC SANDER AND SANDPAPER

VENTILATION MASK

GOOD–QUALITY MASKING TAPE

SCRAP WOOD OR SURFACE

STANLEY (UTILITY) KNIFE

SEALANT/CAULK GUN

WAX CLOTH/BRUSH/PAINT BRUSH

MATERIALS

RECYCLED WOOD, SUCH AS A
   CUPBOARD DOOR

CHALK PAINT

5 PALLET BOARDS

WOOD GLUE

GALVANISED CLOUT NAILS (15-20MM,
   DEPENDING ON THE THICKNESS OF
   THE WOOD)

WINE CORKS

STRONG ADHESIVE, E.G. NO MORE NAILS

WHITE FURNITURE WAX

To prepare the pallet boards, please refer to Perfecting your Pallet Boards on page 12.

01 If necessary cut the cupboard door (or reclaimed board) to shape. Ours is 56cm (22in) square. Sand to remove any imperfections and to create a key (a surface rough enough to paint on). Measure the centre of the board and mark with a pencil. Mask the board on the line with good-quality masking tape.

02 On a scrap piece of wood or surface, paint the top half of the board in your desired colour using chalk paint. Leave the paint to dry and apply a second coat if necessary. Remove the masking tape once dry.

03 Measure the entire board and add an additional 5cm (2in) to both the height and the width. Ours is 56cm, so 56cm + 5cm = 61cm (22 + 2 = 24in). Measure, mark and cut two pallet boards at 61cm (24in). Sand the pallet boards.

04 Measure and mark 2.5cm (1in) from the ends of the pallet boards.

05 Position the pallet boards on the main board so that the marks you have just made line up with the edges of the main board. The pallet boards will become a frame for the main board, with an overhang that will hide the MDF edge. Line up the marks with the main board to create the overhang. Make sure the boards are straight – you could use a combination square here.

TOP TIP:

For our recycled wood, we used an old MDF cupboard door sourced from a retail unit.

01

02

03

04

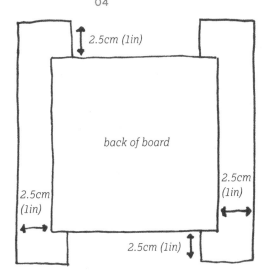

05

2.5cm (1in)

2.5cm (1in)

back of board

2.5cm (1in)

2.5cm (1in)

06

06 Place in position onto the main board and secure into place with wood glue and a galvanised clout nail at each end. Measure between the two boards at the top and bottom. Measure, mark and cut two pallet boards to fit. Sand. Slot these two boards into the frame and secure with wood glue and galvanised clout nails.

07 Using the centre line marked in step 1, measure across the board inside the pallet board frame. Measure, mark and cut a thin pallet board to fit. You may need to trim a board down in length in order to get the best effect. Slot into position and attach with wood glue and two clout nails. This separates the chalkboard and the pinboard.

08 Measure the corks and mark the centre with a pencil. Use a sharp Stanley (utility) knife to cut all of the corks in half in the same way.

09 Apply a strong adhesive to the remaining board with a sealant/caulk gun. Spread the adhesive to create an even consistency for the corks to adhere to. Push the corks into the adhesive, sitting them flush with each other along the entire pinboard. Cut the remaining corks at the bottom to fit.

10 Apply a white wax to the pallet wood with a cloth or wax brush.

11 Paint some of the corks using a small paint brush and the chalk paint.

07

08

09

10

11

FESTIVAL SIGN

Festivals, weddings and events have evolved a huge amount over the past few years, with decor, personalisation and guest experience now taking centre stage. Pallets are a great material to use when creating a specific look for an event. Not only are they affordable but also very versatile, with the ability to create a range of styles with the addition of some paint, pattern and personalisation. These signs are a perfect project to add into the mix as they are both decorative and functional, adding a sense of style when directing your guests. Using basic tools and techniques, this project is achievable from a beginner level and can make use of shorter offcuts of pallet boards left over from previous projects. While we have used symbols with cut-out stencils and spray paint, chalkboard paint can offer even more flexibility, with the potential to change the wording for each event or occasion. These fun and adaptable signs are very popular among our hire collection, and we also use them regularly for our pop-up markets and exhibitions.

TOOLS AND EQUIPMENT

TAPE MEASURE

PENCIL

COMBINATION SQUARE

HAND SAW

ELECTRIC SANDER AND SANDPAPER

VENTILATION MASK

RULER

ELECTRIC DRILL

PILOT HOLE BIT

COUNTERSINK DRILL BIT

CRAFT KNIFE

CUTTING BOARD

GOOD-QUALITY MASKING TAPE

FINE BLACK MARKER

PAINT BRUSH

MATERIALS

1 THICK PALLET BOARD (APPROX.
   100CM/3FT) LONG

4 PALLET BOARD OFFCUTS (APPROX.
   50CM/20IN)

SCREWS

PRINTABLE ACETATE

CHALK SPRAY PAINT

2 PALLET BEARER BEAMS FROM A TWO-WAY
   ENTRY PALLET

OUTDOOR, NON-YELLOWING VARNISH

01

01 Measure the thick pallet board at 100cm (3ft) and mark with a pencil and combination square. Cut using a hand saw. This step may not be necessary as the pallet may already be the right size. Sand until smooth.

02 Measure, mark and cut straight (use the combination square) four pallet boards for the arrows. We did ours at slightly different measurements to give variation, at 48cm (18in), 45cm (17in), 39cm (15in) and 35cm (14in). Measure and mark the centre of the width of the pallet board at one end. Measure 4.5cm (1¾in) from the same end down the length of the board, and mark with a pencil. Draw a line across with a combination square.

02

03

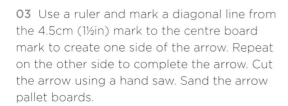

04

03 Use a ruler and mark a diagonal line from the 4.5cm (1½in) mark to the centre board mark to create one side of the arrow. Repeat on the other side to complete the arrow. Cut the arrow using a hand saw. Sand the arrow pallet boards.

04 Lay the arrows on the pallet upright in position.

05 Flip everything so you now have the pallet upright facing you. Pilot and countersink two holes into the pallet upright so that you can attach the first arrow board. Repeat for the other arrows. Screw into the holes and through into the arrow boards to secure.

05

06

07

08

06 Prepare the stencils by printing the symbols onto printable acetate at the right width for the pallet boards (approx 7.5cm/3in). Be sure to use copyright-free images – try free stock image sites such as www.unsplash.com. If you prefer, you can draw your own. Use a craft knife with a sharp blade (onto a cutting board) to cut out the symbols.

07 Tape each stencil onto the pallet arrows using good-quality masking tape. Wearing an appropriate mask and in a well-ventilated area, spray the stencils using the chalk spray paint. Leave to dry.

08 Outline the symbols with a fine black marker to make them more visible.

09 Measure and mark four pallet bearer/ stringer beams at 30cm (12in). We cut ours down to make them thinner. Cut the length of the beams using a hand saw. Sand the pallet bearer beams. Position the first beam flush with the bottom front of the pallet upright and the back one facing the opposite direction.

10 Use an electric drill to pilot and countersink into the beams and pallet upright. Screw through both the beams and the upright to secure using an electric drill and long screw. Continue with the two remaining beams, following the sides of the pallet upright. This will create a stand for the sign.

11 Varnish the entire sign for outdoor use.

09

10

TEALIGHT HOLDERS

The art of relaxation is something that we are all trying to master in our forever busy lives, and what better way to create a calming atmosphere than with these beautiful natural tealight holders. Whether it's for that Sunday hygge vibe or in the midst of weekday madness, these are simple but beautiful accessories throughout the home. Through our personal sales, we know these are favourites with beauty salons, retreats and spas, while also proving popular during the holiday seasons, with many people adding them to their table decorations or floral arrangements. Not only are these perfect for beginners, but they are quick to make, so are a thoughtful gift or token. Try smaller versions for table gifts or favours at weddings.

TOOLS AND EQUIPMENT

PENCIL

TAPE MEASURE

COMBINATION SQUARE

HAND SAW OR ELECTRIC CHOP/MITRE SAW

ELECTRIC SANDER AND SANDPAPER

VENTILATION MASK

RULER

CLAMP OR VICE

ELECTRIC DRILL

40MM (1½IN) FORSTNER BIT

MATERIALS

1 INDUSTRIAL SQUARE BEARER/STRINGER
    BEAM (APPROX. 60CM/24IN IN TOTAL) – OR
    THE BLOCKS FROM A EURO PALLET

TEALIGHTS

TOP TIP:

It is best to use an electric drill that connects to mains power supply here (rather than cordless) as you get more power. Alternatively you can use a pillar drill if you have one. For more advanced levels, use a router and jig to cut out the hole.

01

02

03

04

01 Measure, mark and cut three pieces of bearer beam at 23cm (9in), 18cm (7in) and 15cm (6in).

02 Sand until smooth.

03 Use a ruler and a pencil to create a cross in the top of each piece by joining diagonally opposite corners. This marks the centre.

04 Clamp one piece of wood into a vice or clamp to a secure surface. Use the electric drill and 40mm (1½in) Forstner bit, place the centre point of the Forstner bit on the centre mark of the wood and drill until it is approximately 25mm (1in) deep, or deep enough for the tea lights. Put lots of pressure onto the drill while doing this to ensure it doesn't move from the centre point. Repeat on each block of wood.

05 Sand the holes by hand. You will need a small piece of sandpaper for this.

05

KEY HOOKS

Never lose your keys again. Adding colour, style and a sense of chic into your hall, these fun hooks are sure to get the whole family organised when it comes to those rushed Monday mornings. Using moulded animal toys, easily sourced from the local charity or second-hand store, and a small piece of pallet wood, these hooks are a great beginner's project or a quick and fun afternoon task and are easily adapted to kids' bedrooms, bathrooms or play dens. Change the colours and themes – try neon colours or reds and greens for the Christmas holiday season. Consider the technique and materials for other areas of your home, such as replacing cupboard handles with animal heads, attaching to storage jar lids or through tea plates to create quirky cake stands.

———

TOOLS AND EQUIPMENT

STANLEY (UTILITY) KNIFE/SMALL SAW

CUTTING BOARD

GOGGLES OR MASK

GLOVES

SCRAP WOOD OR SURFACE

TAPE MEASURE

COMBINATION SQUARE

PENCIL

HAND SAW OR ELECTRIC CHOP/MITRE SAW

SANDPAPER

ELECTRIC DRILL

PILOT DRILL BIT (SIZE DEPENDING ON
  SCREWS USED)

CLAMP OR VICE

COUNTERSINK DRILL BIT

SCREWDRIVER BIT

MATERIALS

1 PALLET BOARD

SELECTION OF 4 SMALL PLASTIC TOY
  ANIMALS (SOLID, NOT HOLLOW)

CHALK SPRAY PAINT (IN 4 PASTEL COLOURS)

WOOD SCREWS

2 PICTURE HOOK PLATES

01

02

*To prepare the pallet boards, please refer to
Perfecting your Pallet Boards on page 12.*

01 Cut the toy animals using a Stanley utility
knife (or a saw depending on the density of
the toy) and a cutting board. We cut close
to the back legs, but you can play with
placement and sectioning.

02 Use a chalk spray paint to spray each
of the animals in pastel colours. Be sure to
do this in a well-ventilated area, wearing an
appropriate mask and onto a scrap surface.
Leave to dry and apply a second coat if
necessary.

03 Measure the pallet board at 45cm (18in). Mark with a combination square and cut with a hand saw. Sand by hand. Split the board into five equal sections of 9cm (4in), using a tape measure and marking with a pencil. This will give four equal marks. Measure and mark the width and depth of the board to find the centre of each section, creating a cross on the mark.

04 Use an electric drill to make a small pilot hole on each mark.

05 Use the same bit to drill a pilot hole in the centre of the cut area on each animal. Clamp the animals here to aid drilling. Use a countersink cutter and the electric drill to countersink the back of the pallet board where you created a pilot hole.

06 Using the electric drill, appropriate screwdriver bit and screws, screw through the pallet board from the back and into each animal. Attach picture hook plates to the back of the pallet board for hanging.

03

04

05

06

RESOURCES

Here are just a few of the products and places that make our life, workshop and styling even more enjoyable. Above everything however, we encourage you to shop and support local and small businesses throughout the world!

Homewares and lifestyle

Dr Martens
Work boots
drmartens.com
Various stockists, worldwide

Epanoui
Homewares and gifts
epanoui.co.uk
Bedford, UK (worldwide shipping)

Join Store London
Candles
joinstorelondon.co.uk
London, UK (worldwide shipping)

Lucy & Yak
The perfect dungarees!
lucyandyak.com
UK (worldwide shipping)

Martin & Cox Living Gifts
Plants and pots
martinandcox.co.uk
Northamptonshire, UK

Neat Homeware
Homewares
neathomeware.com
Toddington, Bedfordshire, UK (worldwide shipping available on request)

Pillo London
Cushions and homewares
pillolondon.com
London, UK (worldwide shipping)

Southwood Stores
Scandi homewares
southwoodstores.co.uk
Milton Keynes, UK (worldwide shipping)

Three Grey
Homewares
threegrey.org
London, UK

Tools, materials and supplies

Country Chic Paint
Furniture paint
www.countrychicpaint.com
Various stockists, US

Estwing
Tools
estwingtools.com
Various stockists, UK and US

GH Leathers
A leatherwarehouse that also sells offcuts
leathermerchants.com
Rushden, UK

Harris Brushes
Paint brushes
harrisbrushes.com
Various stockists, UK

Lauren Aston Designs
Giant knitting needles and wool
laurenastondesigns.com
UK (worldwide shipping)

Occuk
Tools including pallet breakers
www.occuk.co.uk (worldwide shipping
available on request)

Novasol
Spray chalk paints
novasolsprayusa.com
Various stockists, US

Plasti-kote
Spray chalk paints
plasti-kote.co.uk
Various stockists, UK, Germany and France

Rustoleum
Paint and spray paint
rustoleum.com
Various stockists, worldwide

Scaffolding Supplies
Scaffolding pipes and handrail connectors
scaffoldingsupplies.co.uk
UK

Vintage Rocks
Furniture paint
vintagerocksinteriors.com
Various stockists, UK

Wicked Hairpins
Hair pin legs
wickedhairpins.com
Hertfordshire, UK (worldwide shipping)

Secondhand

Freecycle
freecycle.org

Gumtree
gumtree.com

Shpock
shpock.com

Preloved (UK only)
preloved.co.uk

ACKNOWLEDGEMENTS

Having both been brought up in single mum families, from a young age both Billy and I have always been encouraged to make do, mend and, most importantly, learn. With both having hands-on grandfathers, individually we learnt a lot about work, creativity and the ways of the world. Later, my stepdad Rod became a huge influence and educator in all that we do in the business and we owe great thanks for all that he has done, helped with and taught us over the years. In addition, our fabulous thrifty mums, with Carol (Billy's mum) an absolute DIY queen (the type that nothing can beat!) and Jill (my mum), a huge collector, up-cycler and all round creative butterfly (not to mention the workshop food parcels). Not only have these two ladies been a massive inspiration to all that we do, they continue to help us grow and develop both individually and professionally. Without these three individuals, we would never have achieved what we have in the last two years and could never thank them enough for their unconditional love, help and support in both the ecstatically good times and the bad times. On a personal level, I can't help but mention the support of my loving Grandma, Aunty Wendy and Aunty Netts who throughout my degree days and beyond have continued to help me and us on this journey.

As a team, both Billy and I would love to thank the second family in our lives, Charley, Aaron and the boys who have put up with us working late into the night, a scattering of pallets across the farm, as well as our odd requests and skip-diving antics. Thank you for everything you've done to help us grow, you've always been a true inspiration to us.

Last but most definitely not least, we would like to thank everyone at Kyle Books and the freelancers involved in the production of this book. Huge thanks to Joanna Copestick for getting in touch and managing my array of initial ideas and excitement, also for teaming us up with the lovely Tara O'Sullivan who has been nothing but a dream to work with. Thank you for all of your efforts and hard work in making this come together and for being such a ray of tea-drinking sunshine in the process, our little Maddie is so honoured to have gained her special Aunty Tara. To Rachel Cross for working her layout magic and putting up with the freezing cold winter in our workshop and to the absolutely amazing Brent Darby, we could never put into words how grateful we are for the way you photographed the images in this book, a man of pure talent, you captured our personality and ways of work perfectly – and even appreciated the covering of dust. A special thank you is also needed for Amy at Pillo London who supplied the absolutely amazing array of cushions for our final shoot, you had us all dreaming of owning them all, and to Agathe Gits for sourcing and supplying the props and accessories. As well as this, a huge thanks to everyone behind the scenes at Kyle Books who I know work tirelessly to make things like this happen, in particular Isabel Gonzalez-Prendergast and Lucy Carter. This really is a dream come true for us!

Of course, there are a million other people we could mention here. We are so lucky to have an array of dedicated friends and family who support and encourage us and our business, you've all had your role to play in making this happen. But aside from all of this, we would like to thank our little Maddie (yes, dogs can read) who amongst the hustle and bustle of starting and running a small business has shown us nothing but love and laughter. We love you so very dearly little lady.